WHEN THE LIGHTS GO OUT

A VIETNAM US ARMY PILOT REFLECTS ON HIS SERVICE AND BEYOND

WHEN THE LIGHTS GO OUT

A VIETNAM US ARMY PILOT REFLECTS ON HIS SERVICE AND BEYOND

FRANCIS A. DOHERTY

AIR WORLD

First published in Great Britain in 2026 by
Pen & Sword Airworld
An imprint of
Pen & Sword Books Ltd
Yorkshire - Philadelphia

ISBN 978 1 03618 335 6

A CIP catalogue record for this book is available from the British Library.

Typeset in INDIA by IMPEC eSolutions
Printed and bound in England by CPI Group (UK) Ltd, Croydon, CRO 4YY

The Publisher's authorised representative in the EU for product safety is Authorised Rep Compliance Ltd., Ground Floor, 71 Lower Baggot Street, Dublin D02 P593, Ireland.
www.arccompliance.com

For a complete list of Pen & Sword titles please contact

PEN & SWORD BOOKS LIMITED
47 Church Street, Barnsley, South Yorkshire, S70 2AS, England
E-mail: enquiries@pen-and-sword.co.uk
Website: www.pen-and-sword.co.uk

or

PEN AND SWORD BOOKS
1950 Lawrence Rd, Havertown, PA 19083, USA
E-mail: uspen-and-sword@casematepublishers.com
Website: www.penandswordbooks.com

MIX
Paper | Supporting responsible forestry
FSC® C013604
www.fsc.org

This work is dedicated to Tim Powell: flying partner, fly-fishing partner, friend forever.

Contents

Chapter 1	Things I've Been Thinking About	1
Chapter 2	Do I Die Today?	4
Chapter 3	Alaska	12
Chapter 4	Montana	16
Chapter 5	The Sand Dunes South of Chu Lai	48
Chapter 6	Suzie Q	57
Chapter 7	Again In the Dark	85
Chapter 8	The Debutante in the Woods	101
Chapter 9	Coyhaique	108
Chapter 10	Explaining Anything to Francis Aloysius…	142
Chapter 11	Mr. Scudder's Houseboat	147
Chapter 12	The Boeing Binder	161
Chapter 13	Nelson's Spring Creek	173
Chapter 14	Lola Marie Galletti	185
Chapter 15	The North Star	188
Chapter 16	V1	192
Chapter 17	Pathet Lao	203
Chapter 18	Finnegan's	213
Chapter 19	That Was Then. This Is Now	224
Chapter 20	Last Words	231

Acknowledgements 234

References 237

Chapter 1

Things I've Been Thinking About

> The problem of self-identity is not just a problem for the young. It is a problem all the time. Perhaps the problem. It should haunt old age, and when it no longer does, it should tell you that you are dead.
>
> Norman Maclean

Weekapaug, Rhode Island, October 12, 2024

The first time I really thought about dying was shortly after I arrived at Forward Observation Base 2, a Special Forces compound just outside of Kontum City, in Vietnam's Central Highlands, which was a lot closer to Laos than I thought I'd ever be. I found out that I'd volunteered to fly over the border into Laos, and that I couldn't talk about doing any of this. Not for twenty years. I promised, and I signed my name to that promise. I never would have dreamed that I would find myself thinking about dying. Dying? I was only 24 years old, barely out of college, healthy, in great shape, full of life. Full of myself. But now, over Laos in a tiny, unarmed airplane, dying became a gigantic everyday possibility. I had to try to bury my fear, to just fly, to just get that day's mission done. Intent on doing what I was asked to do, determined to make the bullets miss, consumed by trying not to die.

After leaving the Army I became too busy living to think about dying. Too busy trying to get hired by an airline so that I could fly big airplanes, and then having to learn how to fly big airplanes, and then getting married and having kids, and then building a house. Years zipped past and kids went off to college. I got unmarried and then remarried and the airplanes got much bigger. And the birthdays zipped past, and then I was too old to fly as an airline pilot anymore. My daughters stuck sixty candles in an apple pie, a bitter birthday because at 60 the rule was that I was too old. I looked in the bathroom mirror and sighed. "What the hell just happened?"

Too old happened. Maybe too old started at 60, but I didn't feel too old. Oh sure, I could teach how to fly large jets for an airline, but I wasn't allowed to fly large jets for an airline. Showing and telling wasn't nearly as much fun as doing, and not being able to do was almost killing me. Love of flying was, is, and always has been, a life-long obsession. Too old? Who says? Who decided that? Not me.

Did too old begin when all the marathons and ten-Ks I had run demanded payment from my knees? When my tired heart misbehaved? Or when my friends from Chaminade High School and the University of San Francisco and the Army and Western and Delta airlines and my parents began dying?

Pages now flew off my calendar, going faster and faster as I began to move slower and slower. It took me a while to realize that slower and slower was not such a bad deal, however. Because instead of rushing along a riverbank, I ambled. And my measured pace let me hear the river tumble and splash, let me marvel at what adept fliers the swifts were as they darted mere inches above the river's surface. The sun that flashed off ice-capped mountains and the pure blueness of the sky that captured my eyes captured me. I had to remind myself to watch where my feet were going. If I tripped and twisted an ankle I'd have to limp back to my car. If I tripped and broke my bamboo fly rod? I'd rather break my leg. Rivers invited me to think about the airplanes I had flown, the places I had been, the almost dying from a barrage of bullets, the triumph of their missing. About the people I loved, and how much I loved them. About a girl I love, and how much I need to love her.

Thinking led to this series of stories. The central themes that run through all of them are love and death. All these short stories are vehicles for introspection, and my stories have traveled with me, some to Alaska, some to Montana, some to Chile. There are rivers in almost all of them. There are fly rods in them as well. Other short stories are set in Vietnam. These recount my introduction to death, to almost dying. Several of the stories deal with older men who showed me, each in his own way, what it means to be a man. Some deal with flying, and my love of it. And one talks about a non-disclosure agreement that, along with post-traumatic stress, resulted years of nightmares and the contemplation of suicide.

My life is very close to ending, and I need to decide how to think about this ending before it takes me by surprise. About how to squeeze every smile out of what's left of it. And at this very moment, if I close my eyes and picture a girl with a widow's peak and hazel-green eyes, I know I don't want anything to end, even when I'm gone.

Chapter 2

Do I Die Today?

FOB2, Kontum, 1970

The colors of back then, the sounds from that time, the smells from those days, they hang not on the edges of memory. No. They live in the center of moments ago. Unchanging over years, constant in their content, unrelenting in their persistence. Refusing to submit to the eraser of the past.

The colors of me are brown. I am brown. My skin is brown. From the sun, and from the earth in this compound that is powdery, dry, and lifeless. It clogs the pores of my face and my scalp, clings to the backs of my hands, my neck, and my ears. I wonder if I will ever be clean again.

The Dak Bla is brown, sluggish, silted, and thick. I can almost hold its water in my cupped hands, so full of other things that it barely oozes between my fingers or slips by the grassy banks that contain it.

The clothes I wear are brown, the trucks and jeeps and tents and sandbags around me are brown. Even my Bird Dog, my airplane, is brown. A brown that makes no statement. It is not supposed to. Because this drab hue is meant to be nondescript, to not call attention to itself, but rather to lose itself in everything around it. A brown that isn't seen, a brown that is just there.

Animal sounds are alarms. When they are quiet, I listen harder. In the mornings before dawn, the chatter of monkeys and birds announce normalcy, no predators, all is well. The absence of their singing, howling, squealing, means that something is hunting and something may move on four legs, or something may move on two. This is a part of the day that is fraught with fear. No noise. The reassuring song of my Bird Dog's engine fades into the background. I know it is there, but its consistent melody is predictable, which makes it reassuring. I don't listen to its monotonous throb. I listen for its missed beat. My engine's missed beat is as frightening as quiet monkeys.

A siren's pre-dawn wail is surprising when it goes off, but my response is automatic. Incoming! Get to the floor, flak jacket and helmet on, my hand strangling the sling of my CAR-15. Crawl for the bunker and listen to the whumps or cracks. Whumps mean mortars, cracks mean small arms, and small arms mean the compound is being assaulted. Whumps scare me but not as much as cracks, because cracks mean that I might see someone, and might have to fire this rifle at someone. And someone might fire back, or fire first.

Even now, when I hear rotor blades shredding the air, I look up. Helicopters. Their sound is unmistakable, a memory inescapable. *Whupwhupwhupwhupwhup*, a rhythmic percussion of metal and air. To a team in contact the sound of our F-4's whining turbines with tongues of flame flashing from their exhausts or the chugging throb of the A-1s' big radial engines shouts safety. Under the umbrella of the attack aircraft, the *whupwhupwhup* of a Huey means survival. The rapid staccato of the door gunners' .30 caliber machine guns means protection as the team climbs on board. The roar of the Huey's engine as it climbs away means life.

Vietnam is a cacophony of smells. The sour smell of rotting vegetation mingles with the sweetness of jasmine vines, a sauce of fermented fish heads mingles with the sharp nasal pinch of ground chilies stirred into sesame oil. Livestock feces fertilize rice paddies, and the air is fouled with diesel fuel fires disposing of the contents of our latrines.

What I remember so profoundly is the smell of myself. Of the brown flight suit that has soaked up the smell of me. A brown cocoon of sweat-drenched Nomex, which is not supposed to burn, so rigid from salt that it could walk to the airplane without me in it. The blanket of humidity that keeps me wet, but never cool. The moisture that soaks the stiffness out of the Nomex but makes its smell worse. A smell of humid damp and sweaty rivers of fear, stains from my churning stomach splashed on me, which made me almost ill. If the water is turned on at our compound, I try to stand under it for as long as I can. And scrub my body without taking my flight suit off, then scrub my naked self. Scrub until I scrub myself raw. Then go after my flight suit again. I rinse it, I rinse myself, but both still assault my nose. Someday, I mutter, I will get clean.

Fear smells. Its odor is stirred into the other smells, leaks out from my armpits, it runs down my back, and drips into my eyes. It rides on bullets that race toward the Bird Dog. It reminds me of my mortality. It demands that I pay attention. Fear tests my reaction time, strains the relationship between reason and response. It shouts at me to move without thinking.

It whispers to me that I would be better off if I don't listen to what panic is demanding that I do. That I just "do," that I should trust the "do." The "do?" It is instinct, reaction, training, fear, and "holy shit." It is survival. And if I trust it, "do" will guide my hands and feet, direct my ears and eyes. It will keep my heart from exploding.

An Air Force F-4 swoops down in a roar of twin turbines, filling my cockpit with the howl of its engines. A big fighter-bomber, it dwarfs my Bird Dog. It launches a series of rockets that slam into a huge compound we have found. Flame and dirt and leaves splash upward out in front of it, and the F-4 continues down. Straight, unswerving, descending. I look for muzzle-flashes from anti-aircraft guns but don't see any. The F-4 continues. Down. The words begin to form. My voice starts to say, "Pull up." But the F-4 can't hear me. Before the words take shape, a flash of orange. The F-4 skips off one ridgeline like a flat rock flung across glassy water. A napalm canister ignites behind it. I see the airplane's nose drop. It bores into the jungle and explodes in a fireball of napalm and rockets and high explosives. I close my eyes for only a moment. I cannot spare another.

Compassion ceases to exist. It has no foothold in combat. It cannot. If I see a face attached to a body, if a voice shouts to me, if eyes find mine, I will have to make the target human. My Bird Dog shields my conscience from the carnage around me, even though it is so close. I can almost touch my enemy. Their faces are unclear, their voices unheard, their eyes indiscernible. But they move, they run, they shoot or shoot back. I point at them with marking rockets; the F-4s kill them.

I think my airplane protects me from accountability. I don't have to hold myself responsible because I don't shoot to kill. I only identify targets. But I am wrong. Because there is a day when I fire a fleschette rocket at close range, full of little darts called nails. This rocket hits a man and turns his midsection into a burst of red. I cannot claim that I am one step removed this time. I fired the rocket, I see him die, and in my dreams, I will replay all of this. Over and over again in the dark, where Vietnam rages, where nightmares drench my bedsheets. Nightmares enough to last a lifetime.

I know my flying partners in the present tense. They have little past and no future tense. If you asked me about Phil Phillips, I could tell you that he grew up in Knoxville, didn't go to college, was at Fort Knox when I was there, and plays a very good guitar. I know that Phil is married, and that his wife has an unbelievable body, no sharp angles anywhere on it. I know this because Phil has a poster-sized photo of her tacked on the wall of our hooch. Her name is Sandy; Phil's given name is Claude. He doesn't talk about what will come after all this. Doug Krout is from Colorado and is capable of sleeping through anything. He is married, and his wife's name is Jeanie. I could be wrong though. Not once does Doug speculate about his future. John Meyers is mostly American Indian. He is married to a woman named Alvilda, is only in the here and now, and is convinced that he is bulletproof. This is as close as I get to the personal lives of the pilots with whom I fly.

Sometimes we share a beer and maybe we eat dinner together at night. We almost never eat in the mess hall on this Special Forces compound, Forward Observation Base 2. It is usually closed by the time we get back from flying all day. So, dinner is up to us. Boiling water cooks little bags of rice and dehydrated vegetables and shrimp. With a hot chili oil that our hooch-maid, the young woman who cleans our hooch—a room not much bigger than a sandbagged hut—gave me. I am the only one who likes it. If we talk at all, we usually talk about what we saw that day, where we saw it. What we might do about what we saw. We don't say anything about surviving. We're here, drinking beer. We survived. Today.

We like each other, but we pretend that we are not close. Acknowledgement of how much we cared about one another happens only years later, at a reunion at the Vietnam Veterans Memorial. For now, we act as if we are keeping one another at arm's length, in a parade, marching distance apart, looking straight ahead. I know what these boys look like, and they in turn know what I look like, but our straight-ahead eyes cannot acknowledge that we have memorized every detail of each other's faces. We act as if we won't risk closeness, because maybe tomorrow a face might be missing. If I stop to really consider this, I know that it's a lot of baloney, a fake steeliness. Should something happen to any of them I would be devastated. I say I don't know them, and yet I have come to love them.

The people who ride with me on reconnaissance flights, the Special Forces recon men, the SOG team members? I know their names and faces and nothing more. I doubt if they know my name because they never refer to me by it. They simply call me SPAF, my radio call-sign when I'm flying. It stands for Sneaky Pete Air Force. That's who I am. To them that is my name. They fly with me once, or maybe twice. And then, in the bloody spring of 1970, the mission changes. I seldom fly with a recon man after late winter bumps into spring. I get photo missions. If I fly a photo mission, a second airplane is flown by another SPAF pilot, usually Phil. Another boy, like me, who volunteered to be here. One of us is about 500 feet off the ground, the high ship, the cover ship. The other Bird Dog, the low ship, has the photographer in the back seat, and is flying with the airplane's wheels almost touching the treetops.

The photographer, using a huge lens on his Pentax, takes hundreds of pictures of what we find along and near the Ho Chi Minh Trail. These supplement and sometimes take the place of recon teams on the ground, inserted by Hueys into landing zones near the Trail. There are usually eight to ten men to a recon team: two or three Americans, the rest Montagnards, indigenous people recruited by our Special Forces. In the bloody spring of 1970 these teams suffered dead and wounded on every mission. Too many troopers are dying, the Special Forces command decides. Our photo missions replace some of the teams on the ground. Ten men on a team; one pilot in an old airplane. My Bird Dog and I mitigate the body count.

I don't wonder if I'm going to be shot at. There is a better than fifty-fifty chance that I am going to fly into AK-47 hell. When I know that I have been assigned to fly one of these missions, I ask myself the same question each time. "Do I die today?"

Brown? Today I own nothing that is brown. Especially not a brown that disappears into leaves and vines and canopy. My eyes refuse to acknowledge that color which once covered me, the everywhere and not-there color. Rotor blades that slash the air? They are not benign. That sound can't be. It never blends into the background music of everyday life. A helicopter will always bring the memory of tracer rounds, bullets streaking red, ours. Or green, theirs. Intersecting bullet-arcs of combat, of rescue, of death.

And sweat? I still sweat rivers. But not like I once did, when the rivers that ran down my back soaked my flight suit with fear. When I reeked of fear. When I tried to scrub and scrub and scrub. Tried to peel the fear-soaked skin from me.

Someday I will get clean.

First published in the Journal for Creative Nonfiction, issue 77, spring 2022. Nominated for a Pushcart Prize, spring 2022.

Chapter 3

Alaska

Shrode Lake, July 2002

My wife Katie laughs, “You keep going back to this place. Don’t you want to see something new?”

“Every time I go there, I see something new,” I explain. The low clouds shroud the mountains. Sometimes I can see the tops, but most of the time they are mist-cloaked almost to the ground. A hundred waterfalls crash down from way up, run-off from the snow. The creek will always be here, changed by winter but permanent in its place. On my final trip to this cabin, I am twenty-six years older than when I first fell in love with Shrode. The same water for twenty-six years. Winter rearranging it, learning it again every July.

Familiarity makes me confident that the fly rod in my hand will find the salmon that I know will be here in the run where saltwater mixes with fresh. I know too that snow and ice will have carved newness into the landscape and into the course of the river with rearranged snags and deadfalls. This makes me anticipate nature’s challenge of rediscovery. The cumulative redesign of a quarter of a century is cataloged in my memory.

The people who have come with me have also changed. My old friend Neil McLellan has been with me every year but the first. We know each other so well that tasks of fire and food, flies and fly gear, housekeeping, and cooking, need never be assigned. Our roles have been ritualized by flying together, and by the passage of time. Neil has always sat to my left; me to his right. I think that if I said "Positive climb," he'd say "Gear up" without a second thought.

My brother Terry and my son Colin came for a long time, and then Terry's job and Colin's life sent them in different directions. My daughter Meighan fished with me twice, once when she was only eight, and then again several years later, a young woman. Katie came once too. Katie, my Debutante.

My father was with me every July until the mid-1990s. We walked the 2 miles to and from the river, and each year I carried more and more of his fishing gear. Each year the walk took longer, and then he told me he didn't think he could cross the fast water to get to the gravel bar. I knew that sooner or later this was going to happen. Anticipation didn't make hearing these words any easier. On the gravel bar we could spread out and swing our flies through the fish as they started toward the falls. Sometimes my father and I would just stand there and watch the salmon work their way up this cascade, not really able to see how they did it. Once they did, it was a straight shot up the river to their natal streams, where these sockeye would spawn and die. I tried to push away the obvious. I could not and would not think it. Except I did. When my father stopped coming with me, I heard the funeral dirge play on my heart.

I tied Dad five dozen flies for Christmas one year. Classic patterns. Hair-winged Atlantic salmon flies. Time-consuming and beautiful. I never saw these flies at Shrode. My father told me that Mom wouldn't let him fish them. Instead, Celestina saved them, and when my father died, she gave me a small package in tattered Christmas wrapping. I knew what this was, and I will never fish them either.

My last fishing trip to Alaska was in 2005, this time just Neil and me again. It had been only the two of us for several years. Neil had slowed and so had I. We still caught fish. We always caught fish. We released two dozen for every fish we kept. Katie said it should be my last time, because she knew that everything had to end, and she knew that I would never admit to Alaska ending. On this final morning, just before the float plane landed on Shrode Lake, Neil and I stood in front of the cabin, taking last looks around. Too isolated, too difficult, too rainy for old men. Almost too hard to say goodbye.

I go to Montana now, to Yellowstone. Fly into Bozeman, drive east to Livingston, and then south down the Paradise Valley to Emigrant. I don't want to go anywhere else. My friend from my Western Airlines pilot days, Tim Powell, lives in Emigrant with his wife, Judi. Tim and I often fish together these days.

I go to Montana now, because there is so much here, and I have a little time remaining before the fast water won't let me cross to the gravel bar either. Some days I fish the big river, the Yellowstone, and some days I drive into Yellowstone Park to fish Slough and Soda Butte creeks. They're in the Lamar Valley, which is teeming with buffalo the size of Volkswagens. Neil will not ever fish with me here, because he doesn't know who I am anymore.

I go to Montana now, sometimes to the Blackfoot, the Clark Fork, and the Bitterroot, to rivers my father will never see.

I take my grandson, and I tell him about his great-grandfather. About how he took me fishing when I was a little boy, just like I'm taking him. How I taught my father how to cast a fly rod, just like I'm teaching him. And I tell my grandson that I love him. He needs to know that because I wish I had heard that more. Now I carry my father in my heart, to a Montana I hope he can see through me, listening so hard for the "I love you" that we both found so hard to say.

Chapter 4

Montana

Paradise Valley, September 2022

We sit in my rented four-wheel drive while a hundred or more buffalo amble slowly by us as they climb back to the top of the ridgeline. My window is down. I don't move, don't make a sound, and don't need a picture of the large animals that are passing no more than 6 feet from my door, with left eyeballs glued to me, eyeballs the size of bread plates. There is a horse trailer attached to an old pick-up not 5 feet in front of us. It contains a terrified horse, who smells the buffalo. The horse begins to kick the rear of the trailer. Its hooves pound the trailer's back doors, the noise as loud as the drum section of a marching band, and then the horse finally settles down after the last couple of buffalo pass. Thank God. I look at Tim and say, "Wow, some of those bulls are the size of small SUVs. We don't have buffalo in Connecticut. Or small SUVs either. Not in Fairfield County anyway. A lot of big Range Rovers. Hedge fund managers' wives on safari to Whole Foods. Not a pick-up truck in sight."

"I just hate losing time to buffalo in the early morning," Tim explains. He takes three steps upstream and casts his dry fly just to our side of the foam line that defines the edge of the current.

"Jeez, have you seen any bugs?"

"No. Not a one. That's so weird. But you know, Francis, I haven't seen many this whole summer."

"Well, there are hoppers in the grass, but I don't see any on the water. Have you seen any fish rising?"

"Nope, have you?"

"No. I'm going to put on a Parachute Adams. Just to see if I can stir up a little action." I open my fly box and then decide against changing my fly.

"Well, maybe not. I'll stick with the Gray Drake. Maybe we can get a fish to come up and have a look," I say. Then Tim sighs, inspects his tippet for wind knots, and starts false casting to dry the water out of his fly. He glances at me. I smile and look off toward the mountains, trying to make out some definition. The mountains are shrouded in wood smoke.

After a few casts Tim retrieves his fly-line and ties a piece of skinny monofilament to the bend of his fly's hook. And then ties a weighted Hare's Ear Nymph to the other end. Normally the length of this piece of mono would be a good 4 feet long. But the water in Soda Butte Creek is unusually shallow, so the length of the mono "dropper" is barely 2 feet long at best. "When did it rain last?" Tim asks aloud. It was weeks ago. In my part of the country, on the East Coast, in New England, we have been hogging all the water.

***

"That meeting the buffalo held on the High Bridge over the Yellowstone this morning was pretty cool, wasn't it?" I offer.

Tim laughs, "Sure, if you like to watch buffalo come down the hill, mill around for a half an hour, block traffic, and then climb back up the same hill. Nothing like spending forty-five minutes not fishing."

I think about the conversation I had earlier this morning with Tim, while waiting for the buffalo meeting to adjourn. Tim seems more closed up than he usually is. He did talk about the end of flying, the change in his life that it made, but not so much about what he had done to fill the void. That's a tough one, finding something to fill that void. To take up the space that a lifetime of airplanes occupied. There's the river, the Yellowstone, and there's this creek, Soda Butte, that runs through the Lamar Valley. And Mill Creek, just north of Chico Hot Springs. They usually offer beautiful trout, cutthroats and rainbows, but not so much today. And fishing? Can anyone do that day in and day out?

Tim goes bird hunting every fall over in the wheat fields of eastern Washington. Every fall, for decades. Sharp-tailed grouse, Hungarian partridge, ringneck pheasant. But Tim's bird dog, Mac, blew out his right back leg's ACL two days ago, so maybe no bird hunting this fall. That's a big disappointment, Mac's blown-out ACL, and it means more empty days.

Tim has always skinned out a few grouse, pheasant, or partridge, dressed the skins with borax, and sent the skins to me. I have been tying my own flies since I started fly fishing. In return Tim gets a dozen flies that I tie for him. Dry flies, emergers, nymphs. Tim has several shotguns which he uses just for bird hunting. I haven't touched a gun since Southeast Asia.

On one of the last days of my visit we launch Tim's drift boat and float a short 4-mile stretch of the Yellowstone. An airplane flies overhead, a Boeing 737, on its way into Bozeman. Tim looks up, then looks at me and laughs, "I always look up when I hear a plane. I always have, and I guess I always will." His smile is too rueful to disguise the sadness in his eyes.

I smile back and say, "Me too, buddy." I have been looking up since as long as I can remember. I suspect that Tim sees time slipping away. So do I. Days neither one of us wants to squander. Too hard to surrender the moments. Too hard to surrender the cockpit. Too hard to surrender the part of life that the both of us hoped would go on forever.

The first time I flew into Montana, maybe forty years ago, the sky was so blue it made me squint and went on out over the horizon for what seemed like forever. On this September morning in Yellowstone, the sky is so smoky, the water is so low, the bugs are so scarce. And time? Time is so short. The both of us know it.

***

The day after the buffalo on the High Bridge over the Yellowstone, I skip going to the park and walk north from my cabin up the dry channel bed toward Emigrant, toward Fridley Creek. The channel used to run not 50 yards from my cabin's porch, and I often crossed it just below Tim's house, and then fished back upstream. It held some seriously nice rainbows. Winter storms over the last several years have piled rocks across the mouth of this channel, creating a dam. The water in the channel dropped lower and lower every year and now there is none. It has become a dried-up bed of river rock, which I walk along, going north, an unexpected and very unwelcomed change. It seems that most changes these days are unexpected and unwelcomed.

A new channel, just to the east, has cut through the woods and jogged into the channel bed just south of Story Ranch. If there is one bright spot in the water's moving to a different neighborhood, it is that it still flows through the Story Ranch. The first cattle drive ever came from Texas to Montana, from the Rio Grande to the Yellowstone. This was Nelson Story's herd, and he was the trail boss. This channel I'm fishing runs right through his land, and Tim, who is good friends with the descendants of Nelson Story, has permission to fish here, and has asked for permission for me to fish here too. I get to drift my fly through history.

On other trips I've had great success along this stretch of water. Big rainbows and cutthroats, big browns and whitefish. All on a fly rod floating dry flies, or nymphs below the surface, through most of the spring and summer, then grasshopper patterns in hot, dry, dusty August. As a matter of fact, I can't fish any other way. Because once I picked up a fly rod, I gave away all my other fishing rods. I became a fly fisherman. Only.

This morning is slow, just like yesterday at Soda Butte. Maybe three fish over the course of an hour. Not like April, when I was up above Missoula, on the upper Blackfoot, and released twenty-five fish. Snowy, windy, freezing despite the sometimes sun, but lots of fish.

I see Tim's old SUV pull into a little cleared area next to big rolls of hay. He's already in his waders and his rod is strung with a fly tied to his leader. He comes to where I am and asks how I have been doing. I tell him the fish are all having lunch and apparently, we aren't invited. So, he sits on a big rock with his wading boots dangling in the water and looks downstream. There is a female moose—she has no antlers—in mid-stream, just below us. She looks at Tim, then at me, and then moves on.

I am looking at the clouds over our heads. Tim glances at his boots, then back at me, then up at the sky, and says, "Anyone you know up there?"

I laugh and respond, "Nobody I know anymore. Everybody I know has retired."

"Yeah, my friends too. All of them kicking and screaming."

"You ever think of what you loved the most about what we did? I mean, we had favorite airplanes, favorite airports. But have you ever thought about what it was that made you say, 'This is just the best'?"

Tim looked at me for a moment, and then said, "Montana, I suppose. Being able to see a sky so blue it hurt my eyes. I loved flying into all these little cities. Billings, Butte, Great Falls. All seven of them. The fun of flying an approach without nine million do this's and do that's from approach control. Just a simple, cleared for the approach, Western. Report the outer marker inbound. Talking to operations going into Kalispell, asking our guy to call Scottie's, to tell the bartender that we'd be over as soon as we checked in to the hotel. What about you?"

"I loved the mornings. Taking off in the early morning, the air so still, so calm, almost liquid. Holding the yoke in the palm of my left hand, as if it was the palm of Katie's hand. The airplane then following my lead. Like we're dancing on air." And with that I paused, thinking about dancing with my wife, who seldom let me lead, and I laughed at the image of my Debutante surrendering not an inch to me, dancing or otherwise. And I didn't care.

"I loved the way the airplane moved in the morning. You know what I mean, Tim? Silky. Fluid. Supple. Smooth. The engine noise somehow gentler. Not growling. Climbing up and up and up, and sometimes through a low cloud deck. Didn't you, at that exact moment of coming out of the clouds, finally get the sensation of speed? That wasn't there before? I always tried to look at the clouds just as we broke through the tops, because that was the instant when speed became real, because we were free of the clouds in a flash. Zoom. Free. That was just the best."

"I loved Montana too," I said to Tim. "Like you did. Like you do. But I loved flying International too. Venice. I took Kate with me every time there were seats available. Venice at night, with the damp muffling voices from across a canal. No car noise because there were no cars. And Paris. Katie with me. Up early to go to the Place des Vosges for coffee and croissants. I loved that!"

"That part wasn't only about loving flying," Tim said.

My eyes sweep the line of bubbles closest to us, looking for rising trout. The line of bubbles, white and foamy, moves along the edge of the current. The foam line is like a buffet, and beneath the foam is where the trout should be. They're there, I'm sure. They just don't like us much today.

"You know, when I finished my last flight with Delta, I told the flight attendants that they were not to say anything about this to the passengers. I was getting off first as soon as the forward cabin door opened after we pulled into the gate. I knew that if I didn't, I'd start to cry. And I just couldn't cry in front of all those people." Tim looks up at the smoke-smudged sky again. Then he turns to me and says, "You too? Wasn't that the hardest thing we ever had to do?"

I shake my head, and my voice trembles a little. "There were other things that I once thought were the worst of the worst. I was wrong though. That was. Hands down." Getting old is hard for the both of us. What I find so endearing about Tim is that he refuses to give in to birthdays. Me too.

***

The fishing that we share sometimes turns into a marathon that neither one of us realizes we're running. Several years ago, in early September, we fished for twelve hours straight. We fished until our casting arms ached. We should have stopped a little sooner. But we didn't. No, that's not true. I think we couldn't. Tim unfurled his back cast and said, "Okay, last time through the run." As his fly hit the water, I lifted mine and proceeded to make what I thought was my last cast. Trout were rising, so Tim cast again.

"Hey, cheater! You're supposed to put your rod up. Last cast, Timothy! Remember?"

Tim looked at me just for a second, then followed his fly as it bobbed along the edge of the foam line. "Okay, okay. Last cast. Really," he promised. A half hour later we last-casted simultaneously and then finally left Soda Butte.

I called Katie as we exited the park through the Roosevelt Arch. No cell service in almost all of Yellowstone. We pulled into Gardiner, the little town that sits at the northwest entrance to Yellowstone and headed into K-Bar Pizza. Pies made by a pizzaiolo who learned to make them at Grimaldi's. On 6th Avenue in New York City. We entered the park at seven in the morning. It's seven again. Just not morning.

"Are you just now out of the park? Twelve hours? Nobody fishes twelve hours except you two knuckleheads. And that's why I don't ever want to fish with you anymore, Fah-ran-sis. You have never known when enough is enough." She had a point, a point I chose to ignore.

***

Two days later I drove to Bozeman's airport to catch my 6 a.m. flight home. Bozeman through Minneapolis to LaGuardia. I walked across the parking lot to the terminal. When I got to the empty rental car desk to drop off the keys, I had to stop to catch my breath. Must be the altitude and the smokey air, I told myself. Montana burns in September. Lightning strikes always ignite the dry brush in narrow canyons. When I got to Minneapolis my connecting flight was several concourses away. I was out of breath again by the time I made it to the airplane. I did, however, have the presence of mind to ask the Delta gate agent if I got a hiking merit badge for hoofing it from one end of the airport to the other.

I called Tim the next day to thank him for a great trip. His wife Judi, a Wisconsin farm girl blessed with infinite patience, unlike somebody else I know, answered his cell. I knew Tim was having a stress test in Livingston that morning, and Judi immediately said that she was right this minute driving Tim to Billings. He was pulled off the treadmill after 3 minutes, and Billings Hospital's cardiac unit had been alerted to expect him.

"I'll call you back when I know more. Probably later this afternoon." Judi's normally calm voice was hurried. When she did call, her voice was calmer, but the worry was still obvious. "Tim's going to have heart surgery on Monday. The surgeon says there are blockages, maybe four arteries clogged. He doesn't want to operate before the weekend, and Tim's in no danger, so the surgery will be Monday. He's sleeping now, so call him tomorrow. You'll cheer him up."

Tim was alone on Sunday when I spoke with him. The hospital was quiet, and he was relaxed. Surgery was scheduled for the next day.

"What was it that got your attention, that scared you? What did you feel, and what did the doctor running the stress test in Livingston say to you as he hustled you off to this cardiac unit?"

Tim began a litany of symptoms. Shortness of breath, lack of energy, afternoon naps. The list wasn't so much long as it was disconcerting. Because as he rattled off alarms, I kept saying to myself, "I've got that. I've got that." Everything he had, I had. It was as if he had reached from western Montana to western Connecticut and said, "Tag, you're it."

Two weeks had passed since Tim was admitted to Billings Hospital's cardiac unit and had a quintuple bypass and I ran out of breath before my flight home. Two weeks had passed, and then I woke up early one morning and couldn't get back to sleep, or breathe, or push the elephant sitting on my chest off me. A Wednesday morning, when Katie raced me to Stamford Hospital. I was taken to their cardiac unit, poked, probed, IV'd, EKG'd, and the ER doctor said, "You have congestive heart failure. And atrial fibrillation. We're going to have to look for arterial blockages, and you aren't going home later." So, Katie stayed with me until about eight o'clock. The sun was gone, my big window that overlooked Long Island Sound had grown cold, the lights of Shippan spilled down to the beach, and that's where they stopped. Across the dark of the sound, across to the coast of Long Island, the red flashing lights at the Asharoken towers winked on, announcing the edge of Huntington Bay, where we grew up.

The IV stuck in my left arm didn't work for blood draws. It was only for putting drugs into me. Blood draws used new needles each time, all into the veins in my right arm. And each time blood was drawn my veins complained. I could hear cheering filtering up from ten floors below me. I was convinced there was a small family of vampires living in the hospital's basement. And every time I got poked, the vampires began to cheer. "Dinner is served, Dracula announced." Night nurse Stephanie came in at about ten, drew more blood—the vampires cheered again—and then she took my blood pressure. I couldn't see the monitor, but I could read Stephanie's expression as she wrote down the numbers. "Am I going to live?" I asked, half smart-assed, half terrified.

"Knock off the chit-chat, buster." Her eyes were bright shiny big. She grabbed the phone, ordered new blood pressure medication, and stayed by me, not speaking, but stroking my shoulder, until it arrived. The new medication was injected into the left IV and after about fifteen minutes she read my blood pressure again. Nurse Stephanie shook her head and made another call. A higher dose. Still not speaking. Another reading. This time I saw her eyes relax. "You're going to live. Smart-ass." A small smile. She smiled a small smile.

Old age means that body parts begin to wear out. Like hearts. Some parts can be fixed and some need to be replaced. I was in line for another procedure that would sync a misfiring atrial chamber, and a few months after the atrial procedure, two new knees. Tim didn't need any further surgeries. He needed someone to listen. To help him cope with the loss of his pilot's license. You can't have heart attacks and then drive a passenger airplane. Tim, who had been flying corporate after retiring from Delta, was grounded. He was really and truly and finally done.

I didn't see Tim until the following April, in the middle of the month. We met two other retired pilots, old friends from Western and Delta, in Missoula. We had been getting together annually to float the Blackfoot, the Bitterroot, and the Clark Fork, fishing an early spring hatch of stoneflies. George picked me up at the airport and drove to the KOA campground. He had his motorhome parked there. Les's motorhome was parked there too. Tim had also arrived and was staying with Les. When I opened the door to Les's trailer I saw Tim, asleep in a recliner. Tim didn't look like Tim. His frame was too skinny, his color too ashy. His face too drawn. We were the same age, but we didn't look the same age so much anymore.

We drove with the guides and rafts south from Missoula, south through the Bitterroot Valley, and launched the rafts in the upper stretch of the Bitterroot River. The temperature was in the low fifties with a little wind. But Tim got cold right away. It was just after ten in the morning, and we would be fishing until around five-thirty that afternoon. Tim was already cold.

***

We've known each other for forty years. We first flew together when we were based together in Minneapolis, Tim commuting to work from Seattle and me commuting from Los Angeles. On the Boeing 727 my seat was to the right of the captain's and my instrument panel was a repeat of what was in front of the captain. Artificial horizon, altimeter, vertical speed indicator, assorted radio-directional pointers, radar, airspeed indicator, and a lot of knobs and buttons. And lights. Green ones for "go," yellow ones for "uh-oh," and red ones for "stop sitting on your hands and do something."

Tim sat behind me and sideways to the front of the airplane. His panel was an organized menagerie of gauges, dials, lights, and switches. All laid out in order, and all grouped according to the systems they operated. Electrical, air conditioning, pressurization, ice and rain, hydraulics, fuel, fire. Every now and then a captain would let the flight engineer fly. That meant that Tim and I would trade seats. He was a really good pilot, but I had to study Tim's engineer panel and think for a moment about what I was looking at. Every now and then I'd tap him on the shoulder, point to a switch, and ask, "What does this do?" Or, "If I push this, what happens?" I really did know how everything on his panel worked, but I loved to pretend I didn't, just to yank his chain a little.

On our very first time sharing a cramped cockpit we flew with a captain who never spoke. Not a word. To either of us. Not hello, not "Howya doin'?" Not a word. I'd read a checklist, and for the captain's responses Tim would answer.

I'd ask, "Radios?"

Tim would say, "Tuned and identified, set for departure." The captain's response. But the captain wasn't talking. If Tim read a checklist I'd answer for the captain and for me. Tim: "Takeoff speeds set for Vref and rotation?"

Me, for Captain Speechless: "Roger on the left side." And me for me: "Roger on the right."

We did this for two three-day trips, flown back-to-back, six days in all, with the captain's grouchy frown making the atmosphere in the cockpit suffocating. Speechless owned a mid-Sixties Ferrari convertible, the operative word here being "owned." Because, so the story went, the last time he saw it, his Ferrari was being driven off by his now former wife, down the road, and away from him. Saying goodbye to the Ferrari made our captain a very irascible fellow. He obviously liked the Ferrari a whole lot more than he liked his ex.

After we finished the first three-day wordless trip, I decided to make things worse. I bet Tim ten bucks I could get Captain

Speechless to talk. Tim looked at me, said, "Oh Jesus, what are you going to do?"

"Just make the bet. I'll do everything else."

"Okay, you're on. But leave me out of this!"

We were already in the Seven-Two's cockpit doing the pre-flight checks for the first leg of the second three-day trip when Captain Speechless arrived. He stowed his suitcase and slid his flight kit into its space between the fuselage and his seat, sat down, and proceeded to glare at the rest of the world out his side window. I completed my pre-flight check, along with his, and then began a conversation between him and me, with me playing both roles.

"So, Francis, what did you do after we got back yesterday?" I asked myself. And then I responded to the question that I, pretending to be him, asked.

"I went for a run around Lake Nokomis, got back to the commuter apartment that I shared with several other junior pilots, and went to see *In the Heat of the Night* with one of my roommates, who did not look remotely like Kathleen Turner. Up early this morning and here I am. How about you?" And then I answered for him.

"Not much. Had a couple of beers with dinner and then tried to arrange a date for when we get back. The lady I asked out suggested I work on my attitude and not to call her until I made some changes." Then, and I can't say I was surprised, Captain Speechless's palm slammed the top of the glareshield. *Wham*!

He swung around, pointed his right index finger at me, almost touching my nose, and said, "Shut the fuck up, Docheree." I did. And I didn't smile, even when he butchered my name. I knew all the derivations. Dawtry with a w, Doddery with two d's, Doughtry with a gh, Dottery with two t's. I couldn't believe that Doherty was so hard to pronounce. Dough—Her—Tee. Easy! Good thing, maybe, that the immigration officer on Ellis Island changed it from the original Gaelic, O'Dochartaigh. If that guy had left it unchanged, then nobody would be able to spell it either. I just might have to change it back to Gaelic.

I couldn't hear Tim laughing because he didn't dare laugh out loud. I had to turn to my left so Speechless could poke his finger at my nose, and then I was able to see Tim out of the corner of my eye. He had his head down. Like he was trying to hide. Like he was innocent. He was once a prisoner of Catholic schools and was very good at pretending to be innocent. I know, because I went to Catholic school too, and I'm great at pretending to be innocent. Facing the front now, I extended my right hand, palm up, backwards through the little space between my seat and the fuselage's side wall, towards Tim's flight engineer panel. There was a little slip of paper in my palm. It said, "Ten bucks."

***

Tim and I fished together just before Covid, in early October. Sometimes October in Montana can be brightly beautiful, wool-sweater comfortable, sunshiny warm. Not this time. My flight into Bozeman landed in a blizzard. Katie would call it "freezationing." Tim decided to stay home on my first full day at the cabin. Overcast, windy, spitting snow, freezing. I drove south, into the park, and then east through the Lamar Valley over dicey roads, to a stretch of river I hadn't explored yet. I needed to be out here because Montana wasn't forever. I wouldn't live forever. I couldn't waste days. I forgot the weather, tramped through the icy snow, and strung up my fly rod.

A line of foamy bubbles rode the seam between the quick current and the slower, calmer water that eased gently into the icy shallows. If there were fish in this run, they would be holding in that slower water that created a seam with the fast. They would be looking up into the foam bubbles. That's where the food would be. Even in this cold, little mayflies called *Baetis* hatched now, on cloudy days. The fish I was stalking keyed on these tiny bugs. The trout barely dented the surface or made a small swirl as they sipped the mayflies.

My feet were so cold. Snow had begun to pile up on the rocks that lined the banks of this river. Small, thin sheets of ice were starting to form at the water's edge. The deeper water was chilled almost to freezing, held open only by the rush of the current. The river birch, alders and pines that overhung this pool dripped both icy raindrops and gray-green moss, casting a shroud over the weak light. The river was devoid of color, appearing a transparent black.

My fly, smaller than the size of the nail on my pinky finger, rode the foam. It had a white wing that helped me see it. Just barely. Because it was such a small fly, I had to use a very light leader, the piece of monofilament that was nail-knotted to my fly line. These trout were "nice" fish. Maybe a fat 18 inches or more. I couldn't be clumsy if one of them took my *Baetis*. Otherwise, the tippet would break, and I would lose the fish.

I sat on a rock, higher up on the bank, away from the water. My fly rod leaned against the rock next to me. Hot tea from my thermos warmed me a little. The sky was darker, it seemed. But there was almost no breeze. A breeze would make it colder. I watched the water. Every now and then there was a slick spot that let me see all the way to the rocky bottom. Like peeking into the river's heart. Seeing the trout facing upstream at the edge of the quick current, holding deep in this run. I loved it when this happened. This chance to see a special, calm place. The wordless quiet of this river was comforting, its chance gift of simply glimpsing fish soothing and familiar.

I cast and then watched my fly drift with the current. It had to float along like it was a real bug or the trout wouldn't touch it. And I couldn't look away. I might miss the slight swirl around my fly, the dimpled surface in the water that so silently announced a "take." I was able to think about all kinds of other things, but my eyes couldn't wander. I raised my rod tip up, the line went taut, and a fish was "on." No need to set the hook; the fish hooked itself as it turned to bolt downstream. I played it carefully for about ten minutes and then guided it to the rocky bank. The pinkish-red stripe down its side, the spotted green back and silver belly, said rainbow trout. I love this species. They came out of the water like Polaris missiles and made my old Hardy reel screech when they ran. My pliers slipped the barbless hook from the rainbow's jaw. I wet my hands in the freezing water and cradled it, facing its head into the current. Pretty soon it was breathing steadily. The second flick of the trout's tail sent it rocketing back into the river.

I have been fishing for as long as I can remember. When I was a little boy, I went with my father and his father, who almost always came along. They would rent a rowboat with an outboard motor and fish along the south shore of Long Island for spring and fall flounder, and for fluke (summer flounder) when it was warm. We were Catholics. We ate fish on Fridays, so we kept the fish we caught. Pa, my grandfather, always wore a suit and a tie and a bowler hat. Very old sod Irish. Dad was a lot less formal. Paint-stained khakis and an old sweatshirt. As the day warmed up, Pa's jacket came off. Not the hat, or the tie.

They fished with rods and reels. I used a dropline, a fishing line wrapped around a stick that I held with two hands. The idea was to bounce the bait, usually minnows or sandworms, off the bottom. I actually caught fish with this primitive contraption. My grandfather said that his grandson always caught fish. That made me feel good, because I wanted to catch as many as my father and grandfather. One summer morning I landed a fluke that was almost as big as I was. On that dropline. I wouldn't let anyone help me. I hauled that fish into the boat by myself and we kept it for dinner. That afternoon, on the way home, Pa had Dad stop at a tackle shop and he bought me a proper rod and reel.

My father always had powdered donuts and beer for us on the mornings when we fished. I loved sitting with him and Pa, watching them drink breakfast beer and eat donuts. And wondering how Pa never got powdered sugar down the front of his suit coat. I was given a splash of beer in a coffee cup along with a donut too, and Dad warned me not to mention what I had for breakfast to my mother.

It was always quiet on the rented skiff. My father and Pa seldom said much to one another. No long conversations between them. Rarely a story told, and if there was one it was my grandfather who told it. After Pa died and it was just my father and me on a boat that Dad either rented or eventually owned, the words shared were sparse and mostly necessary. Words required to run the boat or land a fish. Seldom, if ever, anything deeper. The wordless quiet of childhood fishing puzzled me. And because I was a young boy, and nothing was explained, I couldn't help but wonder if the silences were my fault.

I asked my mother, Celestina, once why Dad and Pa hardly spoke. My mother said that when my father was growing up, my grandfather was not very nice to him. I remembered her later saying that Pa was a real SOB. Strong words from her. I waited but she didn't offer anything more. I never took the question further or asked why Dad seldom spoke to me. I should have asked her about this. One of the many things I should have asked her before she died. Before it was too late.

***

Quiet is normal when Tim and I are on a river together. There isn't much to say. Words aren't necessary. Usually, we are separated on a long run by distance. One fishes at the bottom of a run, the tail out, while the other stands at mid-run. Usually three casts—short, middle, long—then a couple of steps upstream. And when one of us reaches the top of the pool, we move back down to the tail out and start again. The only time we stop moving is when we are casting to rising trout, trout that are coming to the surface to snatch a bug floating on the top of the water. Sometimes, after we fish a run we sit on a log or a rock. Then we talk. On my trip just last September, when the sky was so smokey and the fishing was so slow and the bugs were hiding, we talked more than we ever have.

"How do you feel?" I asked.

"What do you mean, how do I feel?" Tim responded, a note of caution in his voice despite his smart-ass tone. Guarded, verbally tiptoeing, I was wondering if I was going to get Tim to answer. So I started slowly, choosing my words with more care than usual, turning questions back on myself, hoping that if the question wasn't aimed at him, he would be more candid. I didn't want Tim to have his guard up.

"I wish I felt better. I mean, I wish I felt stronger." I turned to face him. "I can still walk a few miles along these rivers, but I think it takes me a whole lot longer now to cover the same water than when I first started. And yeah, yeah, yeah, I know I'm a lot older than when we started fishing together, but I just wish I had more strength. I wish I could go further. I wish I didn't get so damned tired. You too?"

Tim laughs and says, "You got any more of those Green Things?" Jesus, Mary, and Holy St. Joseph! So frustrating, really, trying to get Tim to open up, hoping he'll talk about how much we've changed over the three plus decades that we've known each other. Instead, he deflects. Just like always. Green Things. Goddam Green Things.

"Oh, for Christ's sake. Here I try to ask you about serious stuff, and you run away and hide. You want to know if I've got some sculpin patterns in one of my fly boxes? Of course I do, and you probably still have a couple that I tied you from last year. I gave you at least a dozen."

Tim has never referred to sculpins, little bait fish, as sculpins. He always calls them "Green Things." I know he must have at least three or four. But who could find anything in that rat's nest he calls his fly box? His only fly box. He teases me about the neatness and the number of fly boxes I carry. I don't think eight boxes is excessive. I tease him about him carrying only one box, the one I've nicknamed Miss Piggy's. He knows that I've got enough flies for the both of us that will last the two of us and several of our friends for at least the next ten years.

"Looks like you have a bunch. How many Green Things can I have?"

"Take half of them. I'll leave you whatever you haven't wheedled out of me before I head home and will tie you a bunch this winter. Brown ones."

"Not brown," Tim says. "Green. Green Things need to be green."

"Sculpins. They're sculpins."

"Yeah. Green ones."

***

Tim and I called one another during the winter, after our heart procedures, at Christmas and then after the New Year, with me asking how he was doing and him asking me how many Green Things I had tied him. "Some, and brown ones too," I said, never telling him how many I had actually made. I tied other flies too, a small dry stonefly pattern called a Skwala, and an even smaller stonefly dry called a Nomura. And stonefly nymphs too. Enough for me, George, and Les, and maybe enough for ten or twenty guys I barely knew. Because their fly boxes were disorganized disasters. Because they had some flies, but never the right flies. Because the four of us were meeting in Missoula that April, after heart surgery for two of us, to float the Bitterroot and the Blackfoot and the Clark Fork. And I had something I wanted to ask Tim at some point during this trip. It was not a question for an email or a phone call, or something I wanted George or Les to chime in on. It was something I wanted Tim to think about, to answer, and I knew that he'd positively avoid the subject with our other two friends around. So I had to wait until he and I were fishing the same raft together. The question? It was about defining the end.

That April I didn't get the chance to ask Tim my question about endings. That April, in Missoula, with George and Les around, there wasn't a quiet moment. George hated "dead air" so he made sure he filled every available space, with never a pause in his chatter which would let me ask Tim about what I had been contemplating. My words had no place to go. The first day on the river was windy and sleety and cold. And Tim was fishing with George from the same raft. The fish were there, in the Blackfoot, tucked in tight along the banks, looking for Skwalas. And when the trout hit our flies, they didn't sip them. They slammed them. That was great. Especially for me, because I'd come all the way from Connecticut for this. But the other three? They lived in Salt Lake, or in Emigrant, or in Twisp, which is in eastern Washington. No airplanes from

LaGuardia through Minneapolis to get to Missoula for them. Car rides only. Short rides, of a few hours' duration.

Escape from the weather was easy. It was cold, windy, and raining the following morning, and they had pick-ups, so George and Les passed on fishing and went to a mom-and-pop diner Les knew about to eat fried eggs and elk sausage. Tim skipped breakfast to drive home, east past Bozeman to Livingston and then south to Emigrant. The weather had taken all the fun out of rainbows gobbling stoneflies for these three old pilots. Not for me, though.

I went with Kurt Herzer, my guide and friend, to the Missouri river. I didn't come all the way from Connecticut to Montana to eat fried eggs and elk sausage. Kurt and I put the raft in just below the Hauser Dam, which is above Helena and southwest of Great Falls. We were about 8 miles below the town of Craig, which has three fly shops, one restaurant, a motel (more or less), and no gas station. I'd fished the Missouri here once before. But not near the dam.

On the west bank, almost straight out from where we launched the raft, was a big back-eddy. The river's current flowed north but a point of land on the west bank jutted out into the flow and caused the current close to the point to hook around to the left and flow back toward the dam. Like a big U-turn, a slow whirlpool. Once the raft settled into the eddy it turned with this funny current. There were about six rafts and drift boats sliding along this backwards flow, like a merry-go-round. Because rainbows held in the back eddy. It was like a salad bar of bugs. Not too much action on dry flies. The fish were deep. But a little weighted Hare's Ear Nymph about the size of my thumbnail looked just buggy enough to get fish to take. And they did, even though it was windy and cold and overcast. The water was clear but slate-gray, mimicking the cold of the air, and I was cold. But the fish were big, fat, and cooperative. I made a deal with Kurt about trading off from time to time. When the cold really grabbed me, he had to let me row. Then he'd take my fly rod and cast, and I took the oars, and rowed to keep warm, rowed to keep the raft in the back eddy, and then later, as we drifted toward Craig, rowed to keep the raft close to the bank, where the fish always were.

We were frozen, tired, and hungry. It was dark, we had been on the river for seven hours, and after getting a burger and an IPA at Craig's only restaurant we had a three-hour drive back to Missoula. But who cares? It was a great day because Kurt and I caught fish.

Two new metal knees and then Covid kept me home until last spring. I flew out in mid-April again to fish the three rivers near Missoula. Windy and cold—what else is new, even with the sun shining? In April Montana pretends that it's spring. Snow could show up at any moment. It didn't. The rivers we fished rushed downhill, but the wind blew and sometimes howled in the opposite direction. Often so hard that it almost negated the strength of the current. It didn't stop me from catching and releasing more fish in three days than I've ever caught in my life. And when my guide and I stopped for lunch, or at the end of the day, I made a point of texting George and Tim and Les, giving them the day's weather report, wind velocity, temperature, and number of rainbows, browns, and cutthroats I had caught. Because they didn't come. They all stayed home. Because it was too cold, they said, too windy they said, because it might snow, they said.

"You could die in bed, you sissies," I said.

***

I look up. I don't know why I do. I don't hear an airplane. I don't see one. I just look. The sky is a smoke-filled haze. There just isn't much breeze. A fish rises every now and then. I took one earlier on a Blue Dun, a small dry fly. I don't really know why I tied this fly on because I haven't seen any Blue Duns fluttering over the foam line. I just figure what the hell, it's worth a try. I guess the cutthroat figured it was worth a try too. Tim and I have walked down the dry channel to the Story Ranch. I can see Tim from where I am. He is fishing one of my Green Things above where the new channel joins the old one. The channel is quicker where Tim is, the water hustling by him as he casts the Green Thing tight against the bank and then strips it back toward him. He's picked up two fish by working his fly under the overhanging alders and birch that hug the edge of the river.

Today is Friday. It's my last day here. Tomorrow is September 11, and I will have to leave for home at the crack of dawn. This is our last day to fish together until next spring. If Tim comes to Missoula, that is. I'm going to be there because I love Montana, and it won't be long before Montana becomes too much for an old man like me. We didn't fish yesterday because I had work that I needed to finish. I told Tim that I might be working for the better part of the day on the introduction for a friend's book. He said, "Okay," but that wasn't what I got from the expression on his face. I worked through lunch on the introduction, something I had never written before. It was all of thirteen hundred words that I went over and over and over. Miniscule changes, corrections, revisions. As I closed my laptop I saw Judi, Tim's wife, step onto the porch. I opened the door before she had a chance to knock, and she entered, and sat on the chair near the woodstove. I sat across from her and asked, "What?" Because her eyes were moist.

"Can you stay longer?"

"I can't afford the alimony if I stay longer!" I laughed. And besides, Katie would never consider leaving Connecticut and New York City for Bozeman. She's happy to have me come whenever I want. But she's not going to be tagging along, and she expects me home. Saturday.

"What's up, Jude?"

"Tim's taking a nap now. But since this morning he's been on the porch, staring at the old channel. Not talking. Just sitting."

Just sitting? Like maybe he's empty? Like he's out of words or ideas or energy? Like he's out of life? Without fishing or bird hunting or, once upon a time, flying? I can't help but wonder.

"Without flying he wanders. He looks up at the sky and I think that he's about to cry," Judi says.

"I've got to go home, but if anything happens, you need to call me. I'll turn right around and come back," I promise her.

On the day I wrote the book introduction, Judi said that Tim just sat there, on his porch, or in his front room, in his big chair, looking out at the channel, and looking up at the Absaroka Mountains, mountains so close they look as if they're across the street. It wouldn't surprise me if Tim never really focused on what he was staring at. I'd almost bet that he wasn't seeing anything at all. I had never known him to be so down. The question I wanted to ask him is now one I don't want to ask him. He may have already been thinking it without my asking. He may have already considered options, reached conclusions, made decisions, without my prompting. And I thought that maybe my questioning would be misconstrued as my suggesting. Because he may have already considered when and how and where to die. Like I did once, after the war in Vietnam, when my depression was at its worst. Tim has not spoken about this with anyone, Judi tells me. This doesn't surprise me. I didn't say anything to anyone either.

Years ago, after the war, two little blond girls in plaid uniform jumpers and saddle shoes must have sensed my despair. I don't know how they did, but they must have. Because, years ago, every day, after the war, walking across Spokane's Cannon Hill Park on the way to Cataldo Catholic School, two little blond girls in plaid jumpers and saddle shoes, so little, so smart, so magically knowing, squeezed their father's hands and held them tight, which kept him from blowing away.

Years ago, during the war, I asked myself when enough was enough, how much was enough. How great was the risk I was willing to take? Funny, the context then and now is the same. The context is "life." In the first instance, the question of enough asked me to decide how far I would go in completing a mission. How many times would I thumb my nose at death, which appeared in the form of an AK round racing skyward? Racing toward my airplane. Racing toward me. Back then I was 24 years old, a boy really, and I thought I was bulletproof, and so long as I didn't do something really stupid, the AK rounds were always going to miss me. Now the question of enough, in the same context, life, admits the loss of my imaginary bulletproof shield, accepts the reality of old age, and prods me to come to terms with it.

When, I ask myself, is life fully lived? When, I want to know, have I seen enough, said enough, laughed enough or cried enough? When should I be done? We did slide by this notion, Tim and I, last Wednesday, which was the day before I wrote the introduction to my friend's book, when we bounced along the bottom of a section of the Yellowstone. And talked about life after airplanes, and how we missed flying them, and how nothing could ever replace the wings we once had. And then Tim looked down at his feet, the finality of retirement gut-punching him again.

When I was young, time couldn't go by fast enough. Now it meandered, like the Missouri meanders below the Hauser Dam. When I was young and I had so much to do, I moved as fast as the upper Blackfoot, the river surging over rocks and carving out cutbanks where fish hid. Now time flies by me. I reach out to slow it down but can't close my hand around it fast enough. And it swirls past, like the upper Blackfoot as it tumbles down from its headwaters, roaring and singing and splashing and not waiting for me. Because I move like the Missouri as it strolls downstream below the dam. It's in no hurry. Neither am I, because I can't hurry, even if I want to.

***

Tim Powell, my fishing buddy, died on June 14, 2025. Tim and I shared thirty years of dry flies, cramped airplane cockpits, and turkey sandwiches together. We walked miles of Montana rivers together. The Yellowstone, the Blackfoot, the Bitterroot, and Mill Creek will never be the same. Because Tim won't be casting a fly rod alongside me.

Timothy T. Powell, March 28, 1946 – June 14, 2025

***

Tim's Eulogy, September 27, 2025, Hubbard Yellowstone Lodge, Emigrant, Montana

"There is never enough time with the people who matter" – I don't remember who said this.

Eight years ago, Tim and I tried to drift a section of the Yellowstone just north of his house. The river was way down, so we'd float, then push, then float, then push, then float, then push some more. An airplane flew over, heading for Bozeman. A Delta 737. We both looked up. Smoke from forest fires had turned the incredibly blue skies a smokey gray haze.

"Do you always look up?" Tim asked.

"I do," I said. "I always do."

"Anybody up there you know?"

"Everybody I know has retired," I replied. "Wasn't that the hardest thing you ever had to do? It was for me. I cried. You?"

Tim smiled.

A couple of words exchanged in a drift boat that wasn't drifting on a river where even the whitefish were taking a break that seemed to last all afternoon. That's how the dialogue started. Gradually. Which became a revealing conversation that lasted eight years. It took almost forty-two years to get to this point. Before this, we talked about airplanes, about guys we flew with, pilots we liked and didn't like. And then, after that smokey, rocky, low-water day, a window into my friend gradually opened, and he finally began to trust someone who wasn't Judi or Jesse with who he was, and what he cared about. We started slowly. I learned how deeply he loved Judi and Jesse and Tom. How he worried about growing old. How he worried about caring for his wife and children. And after Tim's tired heart cost him his pilot's license, he almost always told me how much he missed the cockpit. My tired heart played the same trick on me.

Trips to Emigrant from Connecticut were always about fishing and included Tim's partner from his initial training class at Western, George Brennan. Bringer of Jameson's, teller of jokes, sometimes over, and over, and over again. Dinners together in one of the cabins that we rented. I brought crabcakes from home that I made and froze. Don't show up without them, Judi said. At dinner, with Judi and George and Jesse all talking at once, there was no dead air. No space to wedge in a word. So Tim and I just let the three of them fill up the room with the music of their laughter. And I made a point of looking at the expression on Tim's face. Joy.

We had reservations at Armstrong's Spring Creeks for this July. I cancelled them. I'm planning on going to the Big

Blackfoot next spring. Probably in April. Tim's favorite river. Norman Maclean's too. It'll probably be cold. Maybe icy. Like two years ago, the last time I floated it. Tim drove up to fish with me on the day before I went home. There was ice on the pontoons, seats, and floorboards. We froze our butts off, but we caught fish. Maybe George will come. The Big Blackfoot will be a dedication to you, Tim. From now on it will be forever changed because you're not there. But you are.

"There is never enough time with the people who matter" – I still don't remember.

Chapter 5

The Sand Dunes South of Chu Lai

Northport, Long Island, July 2019

Vietnam killed my childhood friend Bill Sansom. He didn't die there, but this senseless war killed him nonetheless. He died on the Fourth of July 2019. In the middle of the day, long before the fireworks. He died at the VA hospital in Northport, which is out towards the eastern end of Long Island. A VA hospital is a dismal place in which to die, but it's even more dismal when one is struggling to live.

In the summer of 1967, after graduation from the University of San Francisco, I was trying to find my way out of Brooklyn Naval Hospital, looking for the hospital's exit. I had just left the flight surgeon's office. A Navy doctor had failed me on a flight physical that would have allowed me to transfer as a second lieutenant from the Army to the Marine Corps. I wanted to fly jets, which the Marine Corps had but the Army didn't. I wanted to wear a Marine Corps officer's uniform, which was so much better-looking than my Army uniform. And I wanted a sword. Marine officers carried swords when they wore their dress uniforms. Army officers didn't have swords. But I did have a deviated septum, which disqualified me from flying pressurized jets. Not the Army, however, because the Army didn't have jets. Or swords.

As I walked down a drab gray corridor, I glanced into a big ward full of wounded men. I looked right at Bill. I had no idea he was a Marine, that he had been in Vietnam, or that he had been wounded. But he had been here in Brooklyn for over a month. Bill Sansom, who so beautifully played Simon and Garfunkel on his acoustic guitar, who was on his way to Coe College in Iowa when I saw him last, who was a soft-spoken bookworm when we were just boys growing up together in Fiddler's Green. Bill Sansom, who almost died among the sand dunes just south of Chu Lai. As we began to speak to one another an orderly told me that visiting hours were long over, and I had to leave. To leave Bill there, in pain, in sweaty, twisted sheets, his right leg in a sling, and alone. Decades would pass before we spoke again.

Somewhere to the south of Chu Lai was where Bill was shot. In 1967, among the sand dunes. Not the jungle. Sand dunes. A funny place for an ambush, I thought. What must that have been like for Bill, I wondered, in Vietnam two years before me, before I arrived in Da Nang in the fall of 1969 as an Army pilot, a first lieutenant. I still saw my childhood friend as a gangly red-headed kid with glasses sliding down his nose. Not a Marine caught in a firefight. Not a Marine whose platoon was decimated among the sand dunes, near the beach, south of Chu Lai.

Everything in Vietnam eventually gave way to jungle. First the warm ocean, then the perfect beach, then the sand dunes, then the myriad greens of vines and leaves and elephant grass, and maybe the surprise of death by snakes and spiders and mines and ambushes. Chu Lai, a Marine base camp and airfield, close by the sea, built on sand dunes, edged with jungle, usually conjured up a mental image of Bill whenever I had flown down from Da Nang to land there, or had flown over from Da Nang, heading south toward someplace else.

I looked down from the cockpit at this place each time my airplane flew south toward Qui Nhon. Where would someone take cover? There were no fallen trees to hide behind. Jungles have fallen trees, depressions in the earth. Places for men to squeeze behind or crawl into. Sand dunes don't. It didn't seem like there was anywhere Bill could dig, hide, or burrow in to escape the bullets. Where could he go? The truth was that there was no place he could go. He couldn't escape the AK round that would kill him.

***

Snow was swirling outside my ninth-floor window on a January afternoon in 2007. Big flakes tumbled in the gusting wind. They moved sideways, and sometimes they even fell up. My room in the Novotel looked over Doksan, a busy Seoul street. I had been working for Boeing since 2005 as an A320 Airbus instructor pilot. I had already taught my students for six hours, spent an hour and a half in traffic to and from the flight training center, and sweated out in the gym the frustrations of instructing kids who barely understood English.

Facebook. It was something to do to fill the remains of a snowy day. I had discovered a page that had gathered people, some of whom I knew, who had grown up on Lloyd Neck. I found Bill there. He was 65 years old, a year younger than

I was. His red hair now snow-white, his face still long and narrow and his eyes a great but slightly faded blue. I studied his picture and decided that I didn't look nearly as old as he did. I needed to make sure, so I went into the bathroom and peered at the mirror to check.

Our conversations were tentative at first, because our pause between words spoken to one another spanned over forty years. Revelations were slow in coming, admissions carefully revealed. Bill and I tiptoed up to the events in our lives, sharing a little each time about the places we worked, the women we loved. Our histories were clouded in small talk, minimized by tangents. We were carefully peeling back the protective onion skin that men used to hide in. We carried on like this for the next several years, never venturing communication beyond our laptops or our cellphones.

I don't remember how I came to know that Bill was here, in this old brick building, in the Northport Veterans Hospital. His room had a window that looked out over trees just starting to push out buds. This was where I found him, in 2015, confined to a wheelchair, tethered to one of those coatracks on wheels that was decorated with clear bags of fluid. Tubes ran from the bags to and from his right ankle, delivering antibiotics and painkillers, suctioning away God knows what. At least he could see trees.

Bill said, "Come sit down. You'll have to move some of that stuff off of the chair. How did you find me? What's in the bag?" I had brought him a sandwich from an Italian deli. I cleared the chair and sat.

I said, "Finding this place was easy. Here, I brought you a sandwich. A caprese with prosciutto, and arugula. What in the world happened?" These were the last words I said that day. Bill talked, in between huge bites of his sandwich, nonstop for almost two hours. Then a different batch of pain medications made his eyes flutter and slowly close. I sat for a moment, then left.

While Bill explained the state of his ankle, I not only listened but studied him. His uncombed white hair, his narrow face shrouded in a week's worth of beard, a ratty bathrobe over a stained sweater, flannel pajama pants, and a right ankle that looked like a science project. He looked tired, and he looked scared. The story he told me was horrific. An AK round almost blew his foot off during that ambush in the sand dunes south of Chu Lai. All but six of his platoon were dead. His right foot was attached to the rest of him by slivers of tissue, by what bone remained after the bullet crashed into it, after he ran on his blown-up foot trying to find cover, after he crawled, dragging himself from one dead Marine to the next, trying to find ammunition for his rifle because he had run out. How, at what he was sure were the last seconds of his life, a company of Marines who had heard the chatter of small arms fire arrived to save him.

Bill thought his ankle was put back together at the Brooklyn Naval Hospital, where I first found him, in 1967. But osteomyelitis, a viral infection, hid in the bone, dormant, waiting. And then, in the early spring of 2015, in a dream, a squad of NVA soldiers dressed up as doctors came to Huntington, where he lived now, in the middle of the night. They grabbed Bill and strapped him to a gurney. One of the soldiers waved a bayonet. Bill woke up from the nightmare.

His hand had grabbed at his ankle so hard that his fingernails tore the skin that covered the ankle bone that hid the virus. The osteomyelitis woke up when Bill did.

Surgeries followed surgeries and bed-ridden days marched through spring and summer to fall. Dead tissue was removed from Bill's wound site. Then bone was transplanted, replacing the infected bone. Later, healthy tissue the size of a small pot roast was removed from his left thigh and stitched into place to fill the divot taken out of his right ankle. Four procedures in all. Antibiotics and pain medications by the gallon were pumped into Bill. The antibiotics combated the infection, and the pain medications made him sometimes loopy and almost always drowsy.

Prior to the surgeries, and just before leaving Northport in the fall of 2016, Bill told me that an old friend from school, from where we grew up, was coming to visit. Francee. I remembered Francee. Stunning. She had lived in Norway for years, and now she was coming to see Bill.

"Okay, Wil-I-Am, you need a little help here. Before she arrives, you need to shower. Not two days before. That morning. You need to comb your hair, floss and brush, wear clean clothes with no stains on them, and straighten up this room." He started to protest. "She's just coming to visit. It's not like a date or anything."

I laughed. "She's coming from Norway! To see you. Get cleaned up. Shave. And no matter what else you do, talk about her. Not about your favorite subject, which is you."

Francee entered a tidied-up room and met a tidied-up Bill. They hadn't seen each other in years. It didn't matter. Not a beat was missed. Francee traveled back to Norway when she had to. She held Norwegian citizenship. Visas and length of stay rules were involved. But mostly, she folded herself into Bill. And he into her.

I followed him around from the minor surgeries at Northport to the giant surgeries at Brooklyn VA hospital, which shouldered up to the Verrazano Narrows bridge. Bill could see it from his room. After the last surgery, rehab at the VA hospital in St. Albans. My Italian grandparents used to live in St. Albans. I found their old row house. On Facebook I gave Bill's Lloyd Harbor friends periodic progress reports, and they in turn emailed him with messages of support. But best of all, I saw Bill and Francee in love, a love that didn't require a mentor, an assistant, a cheerleader. So I stepped away. When Bill finally left the VA hospitals in the winter of 2017 and moved into his own apartment with Francee, I went back to how Bill and I used to be, to laptops and cell phones.

I can't tell you much about Bill's life after Vietnam and before the Northport VA. His history after Chu Lai, up until Northport, is better told by those who shared those years with him. I didn't. What little I knew was sparse, with so many blank spaces. Not much about where he worked or what he did, about who he loved, or who loved him. I never pried. I believed that what he wanted me to know, he would tell me. So no guessing, or taking shreds of information and speculating on my part. I would say that we talked about all kinds of things. That's not exactly true. Bill talked and I listened. His thoughts were like a field full of butterflies. Random, meandering flights of wondering. About whether birds could hover. Whether the teleportation of whales was possible. Whether there was a more profound meaning to *The Walking Dead*.

Fortunately, Bill was prolific in his writing, and in his writing, he shared his fears with a group of us. From his frequent emails, and updates from Francee, I learned that his body was breaking down. Of course, the timing was perfect. He found Francee close to the end of his life. That seemed so unfair. Just when he got free of VA hospitals, in what would be his last soft days of springtime, emphysema knocked on his door. Breathing became a struggle. And caused his heart to weaken. Then Time reached back through years and years and years, to the sand dunes south of Chu Lai, and found his shattered ankle, his splintered bone, his osteomyelitis. And Time, from a day long ago, brought them roaring back to now.

Bill was entering a crisis stage in his battle with emphysema and the infected ankle bone. The last weekend of June had just passed and brought a message from Francee that Bill was back again at the Northport VA. His breathing was so labored due to his compromised lung efficiency that he was only able to communicate for short periods of time. A last resort surgery, the amputation of his right foot, which would rid him of osteomyelitis from the AK-47 wound, could not be performed because of his laboring lungs and his laboring heart. On top of all this, his kidneys were not able to work hard enough to cleanse his blood of impurities.

I spoke with Bill that second to last day of his life. He could barely carry on a conversation of short sentences even though he insisted that he be allowed to try. Because he didn't want to stop talking, maybe because he wanted to use up as many of the words he had left as he could. I heard a desperation in his voice that I had never heard before. The struggle not just to breathe, but not to die.

This wound, this red badge of courage, which Bill had carried with him for fifty years, finally exacted the last measure of this stupid war. Among the sand dunes south of Chu Lai there was no place for Bill to burrow away from the bullets. The AK round that found him always intended to end his life. It did. It killed him. It just took its time.

Chapter 6

Suzie Q

Forward Observation Base 2, Kontum, April 1970

It was April Fool's Day, 1970, and I was flying a reconnaissance mission over the western sector of our area of operations, a very bad sector, the worst of Laos. I had been up since about 4 a.m. and launched alone. Trail recon, flying so low my Bird Dog was almost touching the treetops, looking for flickers of headlights, any kind of movement, truck noise if I eased the Bird Dog's engine back to idle. Maybe I didn't see anything, or maybe the North Vietnamese weren't working today (that would be an all-time first!) or maybe they heard me overhead and lay low, waiting for me to leave. I stayed airborne until I was almost out of gas, then headed to Dak To, to refuel and try to find something in a greenish brown can that pretended to be breakfast. I managed the gas but not the breakfast.

Two Huey gunship drivers grabbed me as I climbed out of my airplane.

"You gotta give us a hand at Dak Seang. It's being overrun and we can't get no Tac Air. DASC [direct air support control] won't spring for air and the Green Beanies are gettin' clobbered. We're all by ourselves. You gotta help us, *Dai uy*," which was Vietnamese for captain.

"Okay. Just let me fill up my tanks and switch out my Willie Pete for Nails and HE. I'll be right behind you."

I taxied to the runway as they lifted off, one behind the other, stubby versions of the troop-carrying Hueys. Flying gun platforms, these helicopters. That's what they were. Rockets, mini-guns, door-mounted .30 caliber or .50 caliber machine guns. Lethal. As they climbed northwest toward Dak Seang I eased the Bird Dog's engine up to take-off power, and as we gained speed down the runway, I let the control stick come to neutral. The tail wheel came up, free from the airstrip. A heartbeat or two more and we were flying. I kept my rate of climb to a shallow 300 feet a minute and left the power up to gain speed, to catch the two gunships ahead of me. To hurry to Dak Seang, where a young man about my age would head up a small group of sappers in an assault on a section of barbed wire, to blow a hole in it, to charge through the hole into the Green Beret camp and kill everyone in it. He almost succeeded.

I saw him in his brown uniform and pith helmet, an AK in one hand and a canvas sack in the other. The sack was a bomb, and he was going to throw it at the coils of razor wire that surrounded this place. I saw him running and flipped the switches to arm my inboard rockets. He was at the head of his squad, moving as fast as he could through a trench his men spent the night digging. I was barely 200 feet above the ground. I fired the right inboard rocket first. Nails. Flechettes. Little darts. Far enough away for my rocket to arm, close enough for the darts to remain tightly packed, like a swarm of angry bees. The lower half of him disappeared in a puff of red mist. His head was flung back, his face tilted toward the sun, his arms spread out from his sides and tangled in the wire. The soldier's AK flew off in one direction, his bomb's canvas sack in another. His squad melted into the trench. They must have because I didn't see them anymore. But he was dead, and I killed him. He was dead, and I saw him die.

I had never seen anyone die. Dead? Yes. Die? No. I killed these soldiers indirectly, called in air strikes on them, had bombs dropped on them, had rockets fired at them, called in nape on them. But I never pulled my airplane's trigger and killed someone and watched that someone die. Until today. I believed this young man must have beckoned to the boy that was me this morning, and the boy that was me disappeared, gone for good. The world would be different now.

***

I looked at an envelope lying on my bunk, waiting for me since this afternoon, after staggering back, sick to my stomach, from Dak Seang. Flimsy airmail paper, sent from San Francisco. And the return address? Of course it was recognizable. Hers. I was surprised to get a letter because our regular method of communication had been by cassette tapes sent back and forth. Newsy monologues. She would talk about her classes at Cal Berkeley, friends from school, the patients she saw as a student nurse, older people that were called special friends. My newsy monologue? A lot of uneventful, unexciting, unscary untruths, outright lies, actually, because I couldn't tell her what I was really doing. On my cassettes to her I made everything up.

I studied the envelope without opening it. Then the siren began to blare, and I was on the floor, the letter jammed into my filthy flight suit shirt, my steel pot on my head and my rifle's sling clamped in my fist, low crawling for the bunker. Mortars slammed into the compound. Some seemed to be crashing into buildings right around the corner from where I was trying to slither to safety. Small arms fire too, ours and theirs. AKs don't sound the same as M16s. The rattle of the rifles was coming from a different part of our compound. Did the NVA breach our concertina? I think they may have. "Stay away from our side of the wire," I muttered. I was a terrible shot with a rifle. Was this goddamn day ever going to end?

Once inside the bunker, I sat with my back against its sandbag walls, barely breathing, trying not to make a sound, but holding the envelope up to the little light seeping through the bunker's openings. It was too dark to read it. I tried to read it anyway, but truth be told, I didn't really need to because I had a pretty good idea of what was written on that thin paper. Something she couldn't say any other way. She didn't trust her own voice to a cassette. I knew that I'd have to keep the letter too. Save it for the JAG lawyer who I hoped could help me with this. More letters would follow this one. Formal letters, legalese, documents to sign. I would, however, have to respond to this letter that I was holding. Just not yet.

***

The North Vietnamese had stopped trying to kill me, at least for the moment. They had packed up their mortar tubes and faded back into the night. I couldn't make out the letter's words because the only real light in here would have had to come from my flashlight. And that got left back in the hooch. I wouldn't have turned it on in here anyway. The NVA may have stopped shelling, they may have backed away from the compound, but that didn't mean a sniper wasn't hanging around in the tree line beyond the perimeter's barbed wire. One well-placed shot could have made my flashlight-lit face a memory, my name a fragment of history. I was barely known and would quickly be forgotten.

The envelope was sweaty from being stashed in my shirt, next to my skin, and now sweatier from the moist grime of my fingers. I folded it and put it in my shirt pocket, protected from the dripping air that let me know where I was. Humidity was almost always 100 per cent present in the Central Highlands. I put the envelope on my bunk and opened my storage box. It used to house Willie Pete rockets. Now a bottle of Johnny Walker shared the space with underwear I never wore. Way too sweaty for olive-drab boxers and t-shirts.

Scotch splashed into a metal cup. No ice though. Who had ice? Air Force sissies, that's who. They weren't as bad as the Navy sissies, who probably drank their Scotch out of cut crystal. With ice. The only guys worse off than us were the Marines. They didn't even have toothpaste. I gulped Scotch and reached for the letter, deciding that I couldn't put off opening it much longer. But I did because Phil and Doug came through the door and slugged down Scotch straight from the bottle.

"We got caught on the other side of the compound. Crawled into the bunker by the main gate. There was some small-arms fire near us. Anything take a hit over here?" Doug asked. Then Phil saw the letter. Pointing at it with the Scotch bottle, he didn't wait for my answer.

"That looks like bad news. Do you want us to leave while you read it? You are going to open it and read it, aren't you?" Phil eyed me expectantly. I believed what I thought about keeping people at "arm's length." But I knew these two. I couldn't tell you if they had brothers and sisters. But I could tell you about their courage. I slit the envelope open with my pen knife and pulled out two sheets of almost transparent paper. The first sentence was like a straight jab to my nose.

"Let me guess. 'It's not you, it's me.' She didn't say that, did she?" Phil asked. "She did, didn't she!"

"No," I replied. "Not that. 'I want a divorce. I've met someone and I've fallen in love. I didn't mean for this to happen, but it did.' Good God." I looked around the room. There were almost as many dust motes floating in the weak light as there were exhausted cliches in her first couple of sentences. I felt like her excuses were going to strangle me so I gulped the rest of the Scotch in my cup and poured four fingers of Scotch this time. They just watched me and said nothing for a few minutes.

"Look, Frank, tomorrow's gonna suck," Doug finally said. "If you get to wandering around and you're not concentrating, then bad things happen. Have a migraine, and we'll figure something out."

"I'll be okay. I'm pissed but I'm good to go. Let's get this mission over with." Except for the letter, tomorrow would be just another day.

***

Ah Suzie Q. Ah Suzie
Ah Suzie Q, Baby I love you,
Suzie Q.

The damn letter wasn't going to let me sleep so I walked out to the bunker line. As I approached it, I sang a few lines from "Suzie Q." The Nung (ethnic Chinese) mercenaries who guarded this compound would recognize me because I always used Creedence as my way of letting them know that it was me. They didn't understand a word of the lyrics, but they've heard me sing this before. I always sang it as I approached the bunker line so that they wouldn't shoot me.

The Nung guard I saw most often on these night-time visits poked his head out from inside the bunker, looked at me, and smiled. Stars cluttered the sky, and his gold-toothed smile flashed some of the night sky's glow at me. I nodded and smiled back. He reached his hand toward me; his palm gently cupped the side of my face. He stared at me for a moment, then took his hand away. The expression he wore said that maybe tonight he didn't see the boy captain he used to know.

Nungs have been in Vietnam for decades, here when the French were here. My friend was probably here when the French occupied Indochina.

"Bonsoir, mon ami," I whispered, thinking that he might understand a little French. I knew a little. Very little.

"Bonsoir, mon ami," he answered. These were the very first words we said to one another. Not in my English, not in his

Chinese, but in French. And then this man who was becoming my friend ducked back into the bunker and took his place at one of the gun ports in the sandbags. I half-rolled onto the bunker's roof, staying as flat as I could. If I sat up, my profile could easily be picked out in the moonlight by a sniper in the not-too-distant jungle. I positioned my CAR-15 so that my hand hit the trigger guard and the throat of the stock, making it easy to grab. Just in case.

As I stretched out on the sandbagged roof of the same bunker I sat on every time I came out here, I remembered a story my Uncle Dig, my mother's younger brother, had told me. Dig always listened to a late-night DJ on his way home from work. Long John Neville, who broadcast in the middle of the night, and claimed that he could travel to Mars on the notes of his saxophone. I was able to see Mars tonight. Long John Neville always made Uncle Dig laugh. My uncle's story made me laugh, and I needed to laugh, especially now, to reassure myself that I was still able to. I lay back, my palms cradling my head, and looked up at the sky. No ambient light here, so the whole of the universe was visible. All of it. Stars stacked on stars that seemed to go up forever.

She found someone, she wrote. She didn't mean for this to happen, it just did. And she had fallen in love. She didn't say with whom, or where, or when. She just said that she was in love with someone else, and that someone wasn't me. That was what her letter said, that that someone wasn't me. I shut my eyes. Not to doze but to squeeze out everything but this one thought that refused to be shoved aside. She said, "I don't love you anymore." Her words turned me inside out. Do we need to do this now? Why now?

Did doubts whisper? Did they sneak up in the dark, wiggle around inside my brain and ask me questions I didn't want to answer? Because the question self-doubt was asking was so uncomfortable. That one question in particular kept hammering away. I opened my eyes and whispered to no one and everyone, but most importantly to myself, that maybe I never really loved the girl to whom I was married. And that I was fooling myself into thinking that I would make a go of this marriage, in telling myself over and over that I would make this work. And maybe that was why the photograph of the girl with hazel-green eyes and a widow's peak was tucked into the last page of *To Kill a Mockingbird.* I didn't feel relieved. I needed to get a handle on this admission, to try to sort out what I really felt. I decided then that I was reacting to her "I don't love you anymore" out of anger because she jabbed her finger into my pride, not my heart. The girl in the photograph was always going to have my heart, I whispered to no one and everyone.

A slight breeze began to move the soaked air a little. The illusion of cool. Thanks to the letter I hadn't slept at all, and soon enough the alarm in our hooch would buzz softly. Softly would wake Phil, who slept as lightly as I did. Our other roommate, Doug, could sleep through anything. Even sirens. Barely perceptible trembling announced the presence of B-52s turning Laos into a collage of craters and shattered, twisted, splintered trees. I wondered if they were pounding the area we were going to photograph in a few hours. Time to see if the water was turned on in the latrine, and if the showers worked. Maybe with hot water. I slid off the bunker's roof and waved a thumbs up to the Nung, who was awake, my friend, who stuck his head out of the bunker I was sitting on. I received a gold-toothed smile in return, then headed back to our hooch. I liked these guys, these Nungs, especially the guy with the gold tooth. He always had a smile for me, and his tooth almost always flashed a little of whatever moonlight or starlight there was. But I wondered if I'd recognize any of them during the day. I had never seen them in broad daylight. They were asleep and I was usually flying from before dawn until just dark.

***

The end of March signaled the beginning of spring, the bloodiest five months of my war, the worst stretch of days, which lasted through the summer, week after week, and didn't end for me until the beginning of September, when my company commander, Arlie Deaton, and I flew down to Qui Nhon, where I saluted him, and then hugged him. I was crying. Because I was going home, I had survived, and some friends hadn't. Once home I would have to deal with the legal consequences of this letter on flimsy air-mail paper that arrived yesterday. But it was only the beginning of April, and I still had five months left in my deployment to figure out the best way to do what I needed to do about her letter. On the roof of the bunker last night, just hours into the second day of the month, staring up at heaven, I decided that from now on I was going to have to be strong enough to get past her "I've met someone and have fallen in love" until we talked this through. Let the job anesthetize my churning stomach. Surviving Laos was going to take every ounce of mental toughness I had.

Anger, not heartache. I was so damned angry because she could have waited until September, until I got off the airplane in San Francisco, and then, when no one was trying to kill me, she could have told me that we were over. In the meantime, she could have lied to me during the next few months that everything was good with us. Lied to me until I was safe home. Lied to me so that I could concentrate on what I was doing without getting sidetracked over a part of my life that had apparently ended. What I didn't know couldn't kill me, but what I was doing could. Especially now, because as the last minutes of March spilled into the beginning of April, the terrible days began. One after the other, with body-bags daily, until September, when I climbed on a big airplane and slept all the way to California.

This damned war had me boxed in, because she didn't know what I had been doing and I couldn't tell her. Flying over Laos was a figment of everyone's imagination except for the pilots who did it. Since I couldn't talk to her about the mission, she wouldn't know how dangerous it was or how deadly her letter could have been. That letter cornered me, distracted me, diverted my attention, interrupted my concentration, and could have killed me. I decided to bury my anger as best I could and refuse for now to hear her words tramp across my consciousness. Don't respond for a few days, see what happens next. Cool off. Stay alive.

The letter, now opened and read twice, lay on the poncho liner that passed for a blanket on my unslept-in bunk. I had to stop thinking about it because today we were heading into a really bad section of Laos. Our alarm went off about two minutes after I crept through the hooch's door. Doug was still asleep when Phil and I left FOB2 and drove our jeep as fast as we dared to the MACV compound to pick up Ben Brown, our crew chief. Ben hopped in the front passenger seat and yawned, "Hey *Dai uy*," to Phil and me, then yawned again. "What time is it anyway?" It was that time when it was too dark and too early in the morning. Phil climbed in the back while Ben rode shotgun. His M-16 was locked and loaded with a full clip of ammunition. Phil's CAR-15 was locked and loaded as well. Safeties off. Mine rested across my lap, its muzzle pointed away from Ben, loaded but with the safety on. The unlit dirt road to the airfield was bumpy, and it took us past the cemetery.

I raced as fast as I dared in the pitch black to the airfield. Ben and Phil had their heads down, concentrating on not falling out. I was concentrating on not running into something that had decided the middle of the road was as good a place as any to stand and wait for daybreak. The little slits of headlights were turned off as we zoomed past the cemetery. We were convinced that someone was in there, among the Tao shrines and Buddha statues, with a rifle, eyes adjusted to the faint beginning of dawn, just waiting for the one time we didn't turn our jeep lights off. So we always turned them off. If I had to pick one place to ambush a jeep, this would be the place. Little pagoda-like mausoleums, shrouded in the murky dark, provided perfect hiding places. We scrambled past this cemetery every day, once in the pre-dawn and once just past dusk, but almost never in the daylight. Our rifles were always loaded, the headlights always off, and the jeep always going near the speed of sound.

We had a photographer waiting for us. A Green Beret sergeant with a giant camera. He would be in Phil's back seat. Phil was flying "low ship" this morning and I got to be the cover ship, the high ship. Phil was going to be right down on the top of the jungle canopy, hard to hit because he would be so low. Me, on the other hand? Me and the fucking letter that I had to stop thinking about were going to be about 500 feet above the trees. Perfect altitude for small arms fire to find me. I should paint a bullseye on the fuselage. Make it even easier for the bad guys.

We had never met this guy. This was his first mission, a piece of information he almost too eagerly admitted. His introduction flew out of him, words crashing into one another in a garbled jumble, and he had not stopped moving, twitching, waving his hands to punctuate his bits and pieces of biography. Moonlight glinted off his steel-rimmed glasses, flashing around like semaphore signals. Phil put his hand on the sergeant's shoulder and, letting his Tennessee accent slow the pace of the sergeant's words, said softly, "We only have one rule. Only one pass for photos. One pass and haul ass. That's the only rule, sergeant. Our only one. Got that?"

"Roger that, captain," he said as he jitterbugged from foot to foot. It occurred to me that the speed of his movements had tripled as we got closer to take-off. Standing in front of the sandbagged revetments that protected our airplanes, what would turn out to be the worst day in my life began. This was a day Phil and I only spoke about one more time. And that discussion would take place later today, in the early evening, when the Special Forces major debriefed us. Forty years passed before Phil and I talked again about the second day in April. Neither of us could let go of it, so we kept this day buried with all the rest of the terrible days we shared. As far as I know, Phil has never even said the sergeant's name again. Ever.

We didn't exactly spell out to our photographer how bad the area was that we were going into to recon. I thought the tone of Phil's voice, in his "one pass and haul ass" statement, conveyed how seriously ugly this part of Laos could be. It was as ugly as we expected.

***

Two small airplanes flipped upside-down almost simultaneously and spun toward the treetops. I was the high ship, covering Phil, so my Bird Dog stopped its descent at about 800 feet. Phil made one more rotation of his spin and pulled out right on the trees. We proceeded west and slipped over the next ridgeline. Phil turned north and paralleled the ridge. We used the sun, just up and at our backs, to look sideways through the jungle canopy. Morning dew reflected off the leaves, the sunlight flashing prisms on the moisture. We were at the perfect altitude to see the vine-draped floor. And to see what we were looking for, amazed at what we found, terrified that people would wake up, impatient to get the hell out of this place.

A base camp, bigger than our own compound back in Kontum, was tucked into the trees, dug into the ground, camouflaged with leaves. The occupants would be running for their AK47s, running for the .51 caliber anti-aircraft guns we knew they had to have, as soon as they heard us. And certainly, they had to have heard us. I hoped the photographer was taking all the pictures he needed and that we wouldn't be hanging around here too much longer. Finally, Phil slid his Bird Dog over the eastern edge of the ridge and into the adjacent valley. Away from all of the guns. I could hear one of the .51s open up, making a *ka-chunk*-ing racket as it fired at us. Phil was still below me, but now in a slow turn. The wrong way, back to the west.

"Oh no no no no no. Don't do this," I yelled. My words flew out the big side window of my airplane, where only the wind could hear them. Then I yelled at Phil over the radio, demanding that he turn back to the east, begging him to turn back to the east, swearing at him to turn back to the east. He didn't. He made a second pass. And I stayed with him because that was my job. I could never leave Phil to make this stupid second pass alone. I could never desert my friend.

There was more than one .51 banging away at us now. The sky became a steam of green streaks. Every fifth round of an AK47 streaked green. Tracers, so that the NVA could see where they were aiming. They snapped as they went by my open windows. My Bird Dog shuddered when they hit it.

"My ailerons are shot out, and I can't turn and there's blood and brains all over the cockpit!" Phil's voice was a howl of both anger and fear.

"Rudder-turn east and don't climb," I shouted back. I could see that one of the big machine guns, with bullets as large as beer cans, was splitting the sky behind Phil's tail. A round from an AK severed the steering cable that was connected to his tail wheel. I could see the cable dangling. Then upside-down, diving, with my nose now coming up until my home-made grease-pencil sight was on the .51, I fired my four rockets almost simultaneously. We were finally hauling ass, but catastrophe, which had become commonplace this bloody spring, announced carnage.

I was able to see Phil ahead of me, bobbing up and down but not zigzagging through the air because his aileron control cables were severed. Rounds must have clipped them as they passed through his wings. I didn't see gas streaming from Phil's wings or mine, so the self-sealing fuel tanks must have done what they were supposed to do. They closed around the bullet holes in them, squeezing shut to hold in the gas that we needed to get back to Dak To. I only glanced at the undersides of my wings. I knew they were stitched up by more than a few rounds. Some had slammed the back of the fuselage too, but they missed me. I didn't focus on the *ka-chunk*-ing rhythm of the .51s. I didn't hear them anymore. Maybe we had flown away from them. Eventually we would be able to climb. But not yet. We needed to cross the border out of goddam Laos.

My mind was racing, dancing around what went wrong. Maybe the self-sealing fuel tanks were the only things doing what they were supposed to do. And the airplanes, they did what they were supposed to do. But the three of us? The wretched taste in my mouth told me that we really screwed up. Phil hardly spoke on the way to Dak To. Phil's words, "blood and brains," were almost the last words he said that morning. I told him that I could see one of the cables that ran from his rudder to his tail wheel was severed. He'd have to use differential brakes to keep the airplane straight down the runway after he landed at Dak To. His acknowledgement was that one word, a swear word more sighed than spoken: "Fuck!" That was his final word.

I called ahead and had a Huey medevac chopper standing by to speed the sergeant to the big evac hospital at Pleiku. I did this because I needed to. Because maybe there was a chance that he was still alive. But Phil's "blood and brains all over my cockpit" signaled the futility of my knee-jerk action. The rest of the way back I replayed that morning in my head. Thought about what I should have done, what I didn't do, what I should never have allowed to happen. Three things. Bad things. Bad things always come in threes.

I knew that it wouldn't do me any good to think about what Phil did or didn't do, or what role the sergeant played in what Phil did or didn't do. What mattered to me was what the hell was I thinking? Why did I go along with what just happened? Why did I let him do that? I should have given Phil an eastbound heading as soon as we pulled off the target after the first pass. I should have roared at Phil over the radio to turn east when I saw him come back for the second pass. I didn't. "Please, God. He can't be doing that," I thought. We swore to one another that we would never ever make a second pass; he told the sergeant we would never make a second pass. But the sergeant begged Phil to go back again over the camp. He pleaded and wheedled and cajoled Phil to go back again over the camp. Phil outranked the sergeant; he could have told the sergeant to shut the fuck up. He didn't. And me? I howled out the window at Phil, imploring him to get out. Phil didn't hear me, the radio didn't hear me, but the wind outside my cockpit window did. The wind ate my words. When I finally did roar at him over the radio, it was too late.

The third thing I didn't do? I didn't find the .51s until they had us bracketed. Until they were banging away at us. Until one of them sprayed the sergeant's last thoughts, last words, last flickers of life in a mist of blood that soaked the air around Phil, that covered his cockpit in bits of brains, a horror that has been chasing me over the years, through the night, where the war was fought, and back into the dark, where my nightmares lived.

***

Thank God the water at FOB2 was turned on that evening. My shower took forever, and Phil's shower took even longer. I stood alongside my bunk, a towel around my waist, my flip-flops squishy with soapy water that ran onto the floor of our hooch, some from my hair and some from my shoes. I held the envelope from Berkeley in my hand, then withdrew the letter. Water dribbled down my forehead and dripped onto one of its pages, smearing some of her words. It was as if the water from the shower, the water that began to scrub the events of the morning off me, was beginning to scrub her off me too. I read the letter again, filling in the words the water splotches obscured. The more I read, the angrier I became. She could have given me her news just before I came home. She could have just moved in with whoever this guy was, lived with him. She was sleeping with him, obviously. I didn't need to deal with what she wanted right now. It was going to take all my willpower to put one foot in front of the other every morning, to climb into that cockpit every morning, to come so close to death every morning.

But this morning, this awful morning, I landed at Dak To just behind Phil. I could see Phil's severed tail-wheel steering cable skipping off the dirt of the runway, little puffs of dust popping up as the cable bounced along the ground. Phil brought his airplane to a stop and a jeep pulled up alongside him. I landed, stopped just beyond Phil, shut the engine down, and ran toward Phil's Bird Dog. Two medics were lifting the sergeant from the back seat. It looked like blood had smeared all over the visor of his flight helmet. As I got closer, I realized that the sergeant's visor had been shot away. And what I thought was smeared blood was what remained of the sergeant's face.

We pushed Phil's airplane clear of the runway. I opened the cockpit door to collect his CAR-15, flight helmet and helmet bag full of spare ammo clips. Phil had his arm looped over the wing strut. I wasn't sure if he was hugging his Bird Dog or hanging on to the strut to keep from collapsing.

I put the letter, a little soggy from the shower, back on my bunk and looked over at Phil. He was moving in slow motion. At least he was moving. Water trickled in little rivulets from the back of his head down his shoulders. We've been together at this Special Forces camp since January. And if you asked me to tell you one important thing about him, I couldn't. That we had shared the insanity of these past months was our only connection. The one thing I could tell you, but would have a hard time explaining, was that I would die for him. Not for God or country, for bugles or drums, the cadence of marching feet or flags snapping in the breeze. Not for Vietnam. These things did not deserve my friend. This war could not take my friend's life. Even if I only knew him momentarily, Phil and I almost died together this morning, in the same place for the same no-good reason. That counted for something. Whatever that something was, it had a whole lot more to do with love than that stupid letter on my bunk.

On my first night at FOB2, at the end of December 1969, Doug and Phil arrived late after finishing their missions, after the mess hall closed, in a jeep Phil had just stolen. Neither one offered any details regarding the heist. I didn't care. It was a jeep, freshly painted bad-ass black, with SPAF stenciled across the windshield's frame: Sneaky Pete Air Force. That made it ours. Introductions consisted of very little personal information, words delivered slowly, sparsely, cautiously, giving away nothing. Don't get too close, don't let anyone see inside.

Did fear ever allow anybody to know anyone anyway? I didn't think it did. Fear demanded my flying partners be kept at arm's length; there was not as much pain if one of them died. If you asked me anything else about Phil or Doug there wouldn't have been much I could have told you. A few sketchy details. A little bit of biography, maybe. But that's about it. I felt as though we had just fallen in for a parade on a very dusty field. At the command "Dress right dress" I extended my left hand out to touch Phil's right shoulder with my fingertips, just as Doug touched mine. Now spaced to march in formation, we proceeded in step across a few months together, always moving a day closer to salvation, or a day closer to eternity. We never knew which.

Phil's given name was Claude, after his father, a career Army officer, and he was from Knoxville, the accent that shaped his words unmistakably Southern. Sandy, Phil's wife, was from Knoxville as well, and they had been married less than a year. He may have attended college, but I don't remember him saying that he did, and I didn't ask. I knew that he would tell me what he wanted me to know. And I was alright with that. Because the understanding was that the less we knew about one another, the less devastating the loss of one of us would be. Doug was from Colorado. I had no idea where or even if he went to college either. I do remember that Doug was married as well, and I think her name was Jeannie, but I can't be sure.

If we talked at all, the conversation usually wandered around the events of the day, what we saw, trying to remember the locations of gun emplacements or ammo caches or truck parks or bridges or North Vietnamese troops, at night, in our hooch, over a few beers, and a dinner of boiled rice and dehydrated vegetables, because the mess hall was always closed when we got back. But we never let on about being terrified. Frightened, yes, but frightened of making a mistake, of missing something we should have seen. Never about sweat-drenched fear. We understood that giving in to it would cause us to curl up into a ball and refuse to move. Giving in to it was not allowed. If I let fear take over, I would never be able to make myself fly back over Laos again.

Talk seldom lingered on the past and never ventured too far into the future. The past could give away too much of us and the future could only extend cautiously forward a day or two, no further. I don't think I ever talked to Phil or to Doug about what I planned to do once I left the Army, and their plans for their futures went unannounced to me. The only story Phil ever told about himself was how, after arriving at his R&R hotel in Honolulu, he pushed the emergency stop on the elevator because he couldn't wait until he and his wife got to their room. I loved that about him.

The idea of keeping each other at arm's length sounded good. But it was never true. I looked at Phil and Doug straight on, unblinking, registering every twitch. I didn't care what they once did or what they were eventually going to do. I cared about them in "my right now." I needed to rely on them, trust them, know that they would protect me just as much as I would protect them. I knew that I needed to keep Phil and Doug alive, defend them no matter what, because I needed them to do that for me. I really would have died for Phil, for Doug. But the rest of this war? It was just so much bullshit. At arm's length? What did that really mean? How was it even possible? In our secret little war, survival was dependent on two certainties. The first was 001534. My Bird Dog. I was sure that that airplane would somehow get me home. The other certainty? A belief that was more than friendship, more than two names, Doug and Phil, more than faith. Devotion maybe? A word that men, or boys trying to be men, seldom used.

We killed piles of North Vietnamese troops. But they kept coming. We blew up their gun emplacements. But their guns kept firing. We destroyed their trucks. But the truck traffic along the Ho Chi Minh Trail was like the San Diego freeway at rush hour. We bombed their bamboo bridges, and they rebuilt them overnight. This was their country, not ours. They shouted, "Go home!" Eventually we did.

***

After the photographer's body was removed from Phil's airplane one of us, and I can't remember whether it was Phil or me, taxied the shot-up Bird Dog to Dak To's dirt parking ramp. Two of our crew chiefs would have to fly here to get it flyable, and then someone would have to fly it to our company headquarters at Camp Holloway for major repairs. Then I flew Phil and me back to Kontum in my not as badly shot-up Bird Dog, taxied to the ramp and slowly turned 001534 so she pointed tail-first towards the sand-bag revetment. Phil passed me his rifle, flight helmet, and his helmet bag full of spare ammo clips after I climbed out from the front seat, and then he climbed out too. We pushed the Bird Dog back into its space, tied it down, and counted bullet holes. Phil and I trudged on toward our stolen black SPAF jeep. Me in the driver's seat, Phil riding shotgun, not seeing anything. He kept his eyes slammed shut. I drove back to FOB2. My eyes were wide open, not registering anything, my head pounding.

Still wet from the shower, the towel around my waist, I reached for the letter. My fingers touched something new, a little box stamped with airmail postage that was hiding next to "Dear John." Now what? A little mailer box with a cassette tape in it. Someone must have picked up this morning's mail and dropped it off. The cassette had to be from her because she always sent a cassette. Always. Cassettes were everyday normal. Not her Dear John letter. She felt that bad news needed to be presented in a real letter. A letter I had to hold, a letter I couldn't erase, like a cassette. This cassette? It had her return address on it. Her apartment's address, across the street from Cal's campus. It had to be her, and I had to listen even if I didn't want to. Because I was supposed to go on R&R soon. Hawaii. Six days. She was still going to meet me, she said. She still wanted to come so that she could explain. So that I could listen. She'd be at Fort DeRussy, on the beach in Honolulu, and if she didn't see me get off the bus from the airfield, she'd get on the next flight back to San Francisco, back to Berkeley, back to whomever it was that she loved now. I played her tape a second time, then loaded it into my cassette recorder and started taping over her words.

"If you come, you come. And I'll do my best to listen to what you have to say. To understand how you feel. I don't want to know the new guy's name or anything about him. That can't be part of these six days. One more thing. Be sure you bring your pills. A baby is not part of the deal."

***

I got dressed in a t-shirt, cut-off camouflage pants (no see-me shorts) and walked out to assume my perch on the bunker's roof. The Nungs stuck their heads out of the doorway when they heard "Suzie Q." "They're not used to seeing me in the twilight," I thought. But they recognized the song, and now they're wondering why I'm here in the early dark of evening instead of my usual pitch-black night visits. I was sure they were wondering about me in Chinese. The tape recording back to her, telling her how I felt about her coming to Honolulu, was already deposited at the mailroom. Once there, I couldn't get it back. Once there, I figured I was committed. Get it over with. Because if I procrastinated, the anger I felt would surely kill me.

I looked out across the naked minefield toward the tree line, maybe 100 yards away, and climbed onto the bunker's roof. The Nung with the right front gold tooth stuck his head back out of the bunker and looked up at me. He studied my face, read the sorrow in my expression, then mimicked wiping tears from his eyes. His pantomime took the place of my English and his Chinese. I shook my head yes, then rested my forehead on my knees. My CAR was on the roof beside me, its muzzle pointing downrange, its trigger within easy reach of my right hand. I turned my head and looked at the black gun. I'm 24 years old, a captain, a pilot, with a gun that I can point at someone. And squeeze the trigger. And kill that someone.

In this almost dark, which is turning to the blackest of nights, I think about Phil, but just for a moment. Because I know he can deal with all this better than I can. He stopped the elevator between floors, didn't he? When he was on R&R? I need to think about R&R and decide if I even want to go.

She was there at DeRussy when I stepped off the Air Force bus from Hickam airfield, and she smiled when she saw me. I smiled back at her. We didn't say much in the cab back to Honolulu's airport, on the airplane to Maui, or on the way to the hotel on the beach at Lahaina. And I didn't stop the elevator on the way to our room. The bellman deposited our bags and left. I tossed my flight suit and boots into the closet, undressed her, and guided her under a shower that streamed lots of warm water. She scrubbed the red Central Highlands dirt from my shoulders, my neck, the back of my hands, my hair. I turned her around, so she faced away from me and soaped her small breasts, her belly button, her ballerina's backside, and her vagina. I soaped her and stroked her and caressed her to orgasm, but I never kissed her, and she never asked me why. I didn't want to think about loving her or not loving her, about being married to her or not being married to her. For me it was too much to deal with. So just orgasms. Only orgasms. I didn't want to breathe her in, and I couldn't allow myself to get lost in her, even for just now. When she left, when she got to the airport in Honolulu, when she left for California, when she walked up the airstairs onto the airplane, she never turned around. And when I couldn't see her anymore, I never wanted to see her again.

***

The Nung guard poked his head out from inside the bunker, looked at me and smiled. Stars cluttered the sky, and his gold toothed smile flashed some of the night sky's glow at me. I nodded and smiled back. He took my hand in his, then linked his pinky finger with mine. A Vietnamese gesture, not a Chinese gesture, of friendship between young men. He stared at me for a moment then let go of my hand. And then this man who was becoming my friend ducked back into the bunker and took his place at one of the gun ports in the sandbags. I half-rolled onto the bunker's roof, staying as flat as I could. If I sat up my profile could easily be picked out in the moonlight by a sniper in the not-too-distant jungle. I positioned my CAR-15 so that my hand hit the trigger guard and the throat of the stock, because death might be hiding in the trees.

***

After Dak Seang and then the photographer, the days all ran together, undefined, and indistinct from one another. Fly into Laos, get shot at, call in airstrikes that counted as shooting back, twist, turn, skid, slip, spin to avoid their bullets, wipe the rivers of sweat out of my eyes, feel my flight suit turn into a smelly wet rag, fly as close to the jungle canopy as possible without hitting a branch or a limb or a whole tree. Death so close I could almost hear it laughing at me.

After Dak Seang and the photographer and the days that ran together, after a little more than a week passed, there had been six days of R&R, whether I wanted them or not. Hawaiian night sweats, and teeth grinding and cursing at the dark, and scrambled eggs, and orgasms—hers and mine. She never got around to explaining to me what she wanted to explain, and I couldn't bring myself to ask her. After six days R&R ended, and so did we. She got on her airplane and went back to school, and I walked to the bus that would take me to a big airplane, the one that would bring me back to Vietnam, then military transports from Tan Son Nhut to FOB2, to drop my duffle in our hooch, and finally to sit on this sandbagged bunker's roof, where the stars seemed so close I thought that maybe I could reach up, grab on, and pull myself up, one star after another, until I reached heaven. And I could stay up there, and hide from death, and live forever.

Phil and Doug were both awake when I tiptoed into our hooch. I took the Scotch bottle and poured us all three fingers into well-seasoned cups. And took her letter out of my footlocker. Under her signature I wrote, "Do whatever you want. You're free to go." Then folded the pages so her signature was the first thing she'd see. So that my addition to her letter would jump off the page at her. I tucked her pages back into her envelope, then into a new envelope addressed to her in Berkeley. I handed my friends their cups of Johnny Walker, picked up mine, and said, "Done!"

Doug said, "Now concentrate, for Christ's sake."

Then Phil jumped in. "Don't let her fucking kill you. Everybody in Laos is trying to kill you, and us, and that's enough."

Chapter 7

Again In the Dark

Fort Rucker, Alabama, 1971

Faces with no names begin appearing in the deep dark of night. Not every night, but at least a couple of times a week. Often enough that I think they are living behind my eyes. Sometimes blurry faces, sometimes distinct faces, and sometimes just parts of faces. Sometimes I can't remember my dream of them, or what it is about, but in the morning, I know that they have populated my night because I wake up with a headache. And my jaw hurts from grinding my teeth. Sometimes I wake myself up. I shout, or yell, a few times scream, and I scrunch my eyes shut first, and then open them wide and peer into the dark, trying to figure out where I am. No clumps of bamboo or tangled vines or elephant grass or wrecked tangle of a Bird Dog means I haven't been shot down. No monkey chatter or squawking birds; only a neighbor's barking dogs. I am in the middle of a south Alabama night, not a jungle in eastern Laos. I haven't been back from the war for very long, and I want to believe that anyone who has seen what I saw must have dark-night-bad-dreams too. The faces keep coming.

***

On almost every mission that had me flying barely above a village's thatched rooftops, people looked up. Sometimes they were shooting and sometimes they were just looking. If people were just looking, they were almost always women with children, and village elders who were bent over from years of working in their paddies. Sometimes young boys stood alongside their water buffalos, and the water buffalos looked up when the young boys who tended to them did. Sometimes the village men stood among the women and children and old people and water buffalo. Most of the time they hid in bunkers, or in the jungle, but if they were present, they looked up too. Everybody was looking at me. I was told by our intel officer that the villagers saw my airplane as an omen. When they saw me, they knew that death was not far behind me. In my nightmares, the faces with no names always looked up at me.

"They are Pathet Lao, Frank," the intel officer said.

The faces that come in the dark are unrecognizable to me. All but one. I know this face, I remember this face from when it was the face of a boy my age, from when this boy ran at the head of his squad, with one hand gripping his AK47 and his other clutching the strap of a satchel. The satchel was really a bomb, and he was going to blow a hole in Dak Seang's razor wire, charge into the camp, and kill as many Green Berets as he and his squad could. Except that before he could blow the wire, I hit him at his waist with a flechette rocket, which cut him in half, which made him drop his bomb and his rifle, which made him fling his arms out and become tangled in the razor wire. His head was thrown back, his eyes were open, and he was looking up at me too.

The dead kept coming. From combat during the day, and then dreams later at night. There never seemed to be a pause. As the winter of my 1970 turned to spring our casualties were an almost daily constant, a parade of at least two or three recon men wounded each time. And every mission run by our guys resulted in one or two of them being killed. When one of the missions I flew included an air strike on a village, the deaths suffered by women and children and old people and boys and water buffalos resulted in a much bigger parade. When we caught North Vietnamese or Laotian troops in the open, the parade became bloody carnage. And these North Vietnamese and Laotian soldiers came in the dark too, the features of their faces obliterated by bullets, or melted away by napalm. I saw them as they shot at me, I saw them when they ran from me, I saw them when napalm engulfed them, I saw them when bombs disintegrated them, I saw them when they spread their arms wide and begged me to spare them.

***

Returning to Fort Rucker puts the faces on hold for a while. The first month is filled with fun. I am assigned as a student flight instructor to a Mr. Donohoe, who may have had a first name, but I don't remember it. I don't think I ever knew it. Instructing in a Bird Dog is done from the back seat. That's where I sit, and that's the seat from where I fly the airplane. There are rudder pedals and a control stick and a throttle back there, but I have to remember to ask Mr. Donohoe to lean left or right so that I can see the instrument panel. I have become very good at flying by feel and by sound. Mr. Weaver, my instructor in initial flight training, taught me to do exactly that. And why the hell would I look at instruments when .51s are hammering away at me, firing bullets as big as cans of Budweiser? I always fly by feel. All the maneuvers I learned from the front seat in initial training, I need to teach from the back seat. As far as I am concerned, I have to be perfect when I demonstrate them, and perfect is tiring.

Nights are different. Sitting at an Officers Club bar listening to war stories? Nah. And sitting at the bar in an off-post gin mill promises the inevitable fistfight. (The "War of Northern Aggression" has been over for more than 100 years. But Yankees are still the enemy and aren't encouraged to engage with the local Scarlett O'Haras.) So, graduate school, in classes that are taught at Rucker. A Master's in Psych couldn't hurt, and school fills the space after dinner. I am studying as a college student again, something I seldom did as an undergrad. For a few weeks, studying and being Captain Perfect Pilot keeps the nightmares away.

***

The colonel running fixed-wing (airplane, not helicopter) training at Fort Rucker has as much personality as a C-ration can of lima beans and cold pork roll. *It's going to be one of those meetings*, I think. A meeting in monotone, and mostly a monologue. How I hate this. And no flight suit for this meeting either. Dress greens only. Tunic, tie, pants with the black stripe down the outer seam, mirror-shined black shoes, and my hat. Silver captain's bars on my epaulets, wings over my heart, and name tag on the other side of my tunic. All shiny brass and stiff starch. I stand there, at attention, in full uniform, in front of the colonel's desk, and salute.

"Captain Francis Doherty reporting as requested, Sir."

Colonel Somebody looks up, does not return my salute, and doesn't invite me to sit down either.

"Get rid of the sideburns, Captain," he says. And then, "Who did you work for?"

"I was assigned to the 219th in II Corps but was attached to the Studies and Observation Group. Command and Control Central at Kontum, Sir."

"And you did that for how long?"

"Just about ten months, Sir."

"Well, you survived, I see. Your record shows the medals you've received but you're not wearing any of their ribbons. I have the rest of your Air Medals and an additional Bronze Star. You've received the others?"

"I've received the DFC and the other Bronze Star. There should be several other medals though. Two more DFCs, a Vietnamese Cross of Gallantry and a Silver Star I think."

"Not according to this," he said, holding the copy of my orders in his hand. There is a list of my medals on it. The ones I haven't received apparently aren't coming. Changing the subject, he says, "You'll report to Captain Mainardi, 3rd Instruction Group, tomorrow at five in the morning."

"Colonel, when I was at Command and Control Central..."

"Don't say anything else, Captain. I can't talk to you about that, and you know it. Put the ribbons from your decorations on your uniform and get a haircut. Dismissed."

"You're gonna have to live with your demons, Frank." Those were the first words my flight leader, Barry Mainardi, says to me. It is only five in the morning, it is cold, this would be my maiden flight as an instructor, and I am antsy. I know Barry. We were in the same Bird Dog company in Vietnam.

"I know what you did, and I gotta tell ya that there's nowhere you can go with what might be eating at you. If you talk to anyone and they slip up and say anything, you're screwed. That non-disclosure agreement you signed might as well be tattooed on your butt, so just suck it up."

"Yesterday, when I reported to the colonel running fixed-wing training, he told me the same thing." I had fallen asleep early last night and when I woke up this morning, I had a headache and a sore jaw.

Charlie Finch repeats Mainardi's admonition almost word for word. I know Charlie. I met him during my first month in Vietnam, while assigned to the 18th Aviation Company, a unit I was with for only six weeks. I asked to be reassigned because I was bored out of my mind flying DeHavilland Otters up and down the coast from Da Nang. On one of my last missions for the 18th, my copilot and I left Dong Ha, a Special Forces camp right on the DMZ, on a drizzly September afternoon after dropping off cargo and several passengers, and headed south, back to home base. It was raining hard when we took off to return, raining harder as we tried to climb, and when I realized that only an idiot would fly in that downpour, I descended low enough to be clear of the rain clouds, and to land on the beach if I had to. We dodged rain squalls as far as Phu Bai, a few miles, a harbor full of sharks, and a few mountains north of where my clothes and bunk and toothbrush were. This was as far as either one of us wanted to go, so the copilot called Phu Bai tower to get the runway lights turned up full bright.

"Sir, the airfield is closed."

"Phu Bai tower, we're declaring an emergency. We'll be on the ground in about two minutes."

"Okay, sir. The crash trucks will be standing by."

The copilot smiled at me and said, "You're not planning on crashing, are you?"

Then we skimmed the tops of the sand dunes to the runway threshold, landed, and were greeted by Lieutenant Colonel Airfield Boss, who wanted to know, "How the hell could we be so stupid to try to fly in weather like this."

We found our way to the orderly room of the Bird Dog company that operated out of Phu Bai. The company first sergeant showed us where to bunk for the night, got us fed and even gave us each a toothbrush and a towel. We could shower and put our smelly flight suits back on. Charlie Finch walked into the little office, introduced himself, said the weather sucked, then asked how we two screwballs managed to get here?

And here he is again, at Rucker, standing beside Barry, in the 3rd Instruction Group classroom on my first day as an instructor, telling me that there is nowhere to go with what I had done or what I had seen. Don't talk. Don't hint. Just shut up. We can't go near what we did. Charlie was involved in the same sneaky stuff that I was. There were two of us there with secrets. And the next morning, when my alarm goes off at 3:30 a.m., for the first time in a week I don't have a headache and my jaw isn't sore. Charlie Finch leaves a few weeks after I start. His time in the Army is over. He is gone. No bands, no parades, just gone. And whatever secrets he has, he takes them with him and leaves me alone with mine.

The dreams keep coming, now at irregular intervals. And they change. The faces of the people from the village, the young man with the explosive satchel, the napalmed and bombed soldiers we caught in the middle of a clearing, they still come in the dark. But sometimes my airplane is on fire, and I can't get out. Sometimes I am captured, and a bayonet is beginning to cut off one of my fingers. Sometimes a bullet tears into my leg and my blood splashes all over the cockpit. And sometimes I don't remember these dreams at all, but my aching jaw tells me when I have them.

Leaving the Army makes no difference. Going to work for the airline makes no difference. In fact, the stress of the mid-1970s fuel crisis and then airline deregulation in the early 1980s makes me feel like I am living in a pressure cooker. Am I going to get furloughed? Is the airline going to file for bankruptcy? Is it going to go out of business? Should I switch airlines, which would mean going to the bottom of a new company's seniority list? Then come the pay cuts. And moving backwards from copilot to flight engineer, because Western drops routes, furloughs junior pilots, and reduces frequency on the routes they do keep. I finish writing checks for all my normal expenses that first month of less money. I have four dollars left.

***

A "For Sale" sign is pounded into the lawn, and it takes about two months for our Westlake house to sell. My neighbors there are in business or practice law or have a landscaping company or wear a policeman's uniform or fix people's teeth. But not one of them has fired a CAR15 at another human being or attacked a bunker or thrown a grenade or been shot at or mortared in the early morning dark. I am the only one. Just me.

When the contract of sale is signed, I find a tiny Craftsman bungalow a block from the ocean in Venice Beach. The house is so close to our neighbor that we can pass things to one another just by opening our kitchen windows. Only a few days ago my wife, two daughters, and I had lived in Westlake. The girls had their own rooms, flowers and trees, and grassy front and back yards. In Venice their play area isn't much bigger than a postage stamp and there are hookers on the corners and drug sales on the bike path. There is a guy with a turban on his head cruising around on roller skates, pretending to play an electric guitar, and another guy with long brown hair and a flowing white robe who walks along the bike path every morning. And me? I am enveloped by resentment, embarrassed by having to move my family from sedate suburbia to Bizzarro Beach.

Police helicopters orbit overhead every night. Their searchlights splash into every crevice and crawlspace. Their rotor blades beat the air over our little house. They make the same *whupwhupwhupwhupwhup* that Hueys made over Laos's jungled mountains. The thrashing of the rotor blades and the sweep of the searchlights keep me up at night. When I finally drift off to sleep, the sound of the rotor blades ushers in the faces.

Everything in the bungalow has remained unchanged since the day it was built. The wiring and the plumbing and the kitchen and bathroom date back to 1908. The restoration takes two years. That is because my two hands are the only hands doing the work. But I take out all the permits and just keep at it, then sell the beach house for almost twice what I originally paid. And in 1985 we move to eastern Washington. The people who farm here refer to this vast prairie as the Palouse.

When I get lonely for the Venice bungalow, I just stand in the garage of the Spokane house, because they are about the same size, but this Spokane Victorian cost about a third of what my buyer paid for the Venice bungalow. The garage and the den at the rear are new, but the original structure is a turn of the century Queen Anne, all quarter-sawn oak woodwork, leaded glass pocket doors, a sleeping porch off the master bedroom and a claw-foot tub in the third-floor bathroom. We live on Cannon Hill Park, which has a pond and trees and caroling at Christmas. I can walk my girls to Cataldo Catholic School, just across the park, every morning when I am not flying. And I do. Not only because I want to, but because I have to. I hold tight to their hands, because their hands are keeping me alive.

The author Zane Gray called eastern Washington a desert of wheat. The land isn't flat; it dips and rises then dips again all the way to as far as I can see, and the breeze that is always there dances with the acres of wheat, which sway to music I can't hear because Fairchild Air Force Base is a few miles west of

Spokane's downtown, and B-52s live there. They drown out the music the wind plays, the music the wheat dances to. These are the same giant bombers that sometimes shook my bunk when they flew over Kontum in the hours around midnight and created a moonscape of desolation out of eastern Laos. Sometimes I was able to hear the rumble of their bombs. Sometimes, in the almost light of morning, I flew just off to the side of their target. And after the last bomb exploded, I crisscrossed the cratered ground and the photographer in my back seat took pictures of the shattered earth, of the shattered bodies that had burrowed into the earth, trying to dig down deep enough to escape the bombs. Sometimes the digging was deep enough, and after the last bomb fell, those who survived erupted out of the earth like murderous wasps. The first thing they saw was my Bird Dog, and then me.

***

The bombers and the bombs, the geysers of flame and dirt, the NVA uprooted from the earth by the B-52s? They now crowd into my dreams along with the faces. The war is getting sharper and louder in the dark, and I still have nowhere to go with the dreams. The non-disclosure agreement? I signed it in 1969. Six more years. No talking for six more years. I needed to hang on for six more years, until my promise of silence would expire. The headaches and the aching jaw are every morning now, because the battle I fight in my dreams rages every night. And every night I see the sapper, the boy with the bomb. His eyes look at me from his dead face. His dead hands motion to me to follow him. And all the faces? They want to know why I survived, and they didn't. I wonder about that myself.

The Spokane River rushes right through the middle of the city. There are swans gracing the river's entry at the east end of town, and the river moves at a quick pace until it enters the center of the city. From here it sprints until it reaches the edge of a waterfall, then it surges over the stoney riverbed and crashes down over 100 feet. The river provides a rhythm in the city that is always present, that almost fades into the background because it is constant, and familiar, and expected. Only seeing the falls gives the viewer an appreciation of the falls' force and power. Route 2 parallels the river from the west side of Spokane to the point where the river turns southwest to join the Columbia. The Meenach Bridge crosses the river high above the bottom of the falls, and mist is present on even the sunniest days. The bridge is Depression-era old and the stone guardrails on either side are very low. I picture an early winter morning, with black ice, with no traffic. A skidding blue jeep hitting the low wall. The jeep and I would be airborne, then wet, and I would join the faces. Then the dreams would end.

The question I ask myself is, do I have the courage to act? I decide that that bridge has nothing to do with the courage to do what I contemplate. I drive over it two to three times a week for five years. I look at the bridge. I think about hitting the low wall. But I never steer into it. I still struggle with the faces, but as depressed as I feel, I never do it. Why? Because I realize that the bridge is never going to be the thing that saves me.

In the mid-1980s Western begins to slowly pull out of its financial nosedive. I am reinstated as a first officer on the

Boeing 737, and within a few months Delta merges Western into itself. I have some job security again, and a little more money. But the most important change for me is getting back into the right seat. No more flight engineer. No more sitting behind the captain and the first officer, relegated to the math of take-off and landing weights, and systems management, and not flying, just watching. I get to fly the jet again, to do what I love. I never ask to turn off the autopilot. The instant we begin to descend for landing, I turn that damn thing off. And not too much later, I have the opportunity to check out as a captain on the McDonnell Douglas MD88. All I have to do is pass two written exams and a three-hour oral exam on how everything on that airplane works, then fly my way through a two-hour check ride, where the examiner can break all sorts of things. Hydraulic leaks, an engine that catches on fire right at take-off or a landing gear that doesn't come down. I never think of these as anything more than the biggest exam of my life. I study my butt off, and my mornings are without headaches and aching jaws.

***

The changes in my life ease the pounding head and grinding teeth, but they aren't what save me. Two little girls do. Meighan and Alanna. We walk to and from school together almost every day when I am home. I take them to Lake Mary Ronan, just west of Flathead Lake, in western Montana, where we stay in a little log cabin and make pancakes for breakfast and rent a boat and fish for cutthroat and rainbow trout. I teach them how to cast their fly rods, remove a splinter from Alanna's foot with a tiny fishhook instead of a needle, cheer when they land a fish and cheer again when they remember our rule, that we always release them, and almost fall out of the boat laughing when Meighan names a fish she catches "Rainbow Bright" and Alanna calls the next one she catches "Miss Bianca." I show them the night-sky pictures that the stars make, and they ask me how I know about "star pictures." I say that I learned about them in a far-away land that I will tell them about someday. I look at them and know that I could never leave them because I am part of why they are here in this world to begin with. I look at them and realize how much they have to teach me. I look at them and know that abandoning them, besides being selfish, is unforgivable cowardice. I look at them and rub tears from my eyes when they say, "Read us *Max and His Wolf Suit*."

I look at them and whisper only to myself, "Thank you for keeping me here." I look at them and see that the sun has created halos around the gold of their hair.

The non-disclosure oath expired in 1990. I think that maybe because I have been quiet for so long, the silence is normal. Cockpits have been shared with men who have flown during the Second World War, during Korea. They say nothing. My contemporaries at the airline? We share a similar history, the same war. Nobody speaks about that war very much. I don't either.

***

On a bright October day in 2013, Katie and I cross the Hudson River at Bear Mountain on our way to the cemetery at West

Point. The bridge over the river, the Purple Heart Veterans Memorial Bridge, which was opened in 1924, was the longest suspension bridge of its time and served as a model for the George Washington and Golden Gate. Katie is no lover of very high bridges and doesn't open her eyes until we are across it. She says she thinks she should get a medal for having to endure the torture of this crossing.

The Hudson is almost a mile wide here at the bridge's base, and the Adirondacks soar above the bridge's expanse. The current hurries downstream at the center of the river as it rushes toward Manhattan, and the sun flashes off the current's roiled water. The river here has cut a deep swath through these mountains as it makes its way to New York Harbor. And oaks, maples, burning bush and sumac, glorious in their fall colors, crowd the hillsides that climb toward the military academy, announcing that autumn is fully here.

A cold breeze blows up from the river valley, rattling the gold and red leaves which join us in somber celebration of the life of Captain John Pappas. He would have been almost 69 now. We were boys when we flew together years ago over the Plei Trap Valley, when we almost died together years ago during the NVA's attack on the Special Forces camp at Polei Kleng. John and I avoided the bullets above Polei Kleng, but lung cancer does to John what the AK47s could not do. It ends the life of someone I love.

So, on a brisk Sunday afternoon, Katie and I stand in the academy's cemetery among the headstones of old and not so old soldiers, of fathers and sons, of generals and lieutenants. Off to the side of the gravesite, seven soldiers, an honor guard, all gold epaulets and braid and dress blue uniforms, stand at parade rest, their rifles oiled and waxed to gleaming. The rifles are shouldered and fired. A twenty-one-gun salute that makes everyone flinch each time the rifles sound.

A bugle is played, and the notes of "Taps" wend their way through the mourners that are gathered here. The mourners clutch white roses that they place on John's casket while the bugle weeps the hymn. And me? The hymn makes me weep. Katie reaches for my hand. I close my eyes. I feel John standing next to me and decide to tell the story. And hope that by telling the story I will find peace.

Once home, I retrieve my medals from the back of the drawer they have been hiding in for years. Katie takes the Distinguished Flying Cross from me and cradles it gently in the palm of her hand. A bronze propeller suspended from a red, white and blue ribbon.

"Why did you get this?"

Words I have held back for decades now spill out. I tell her about terrible days, then cover my tears with the palms of my hands. And in the dark behind my hands, I see new faces. Not the dead, but little girl faces. Meighan and Alanna, who have given me all the reason I will ever need to live. My little girls, who save me over and over again.

Chapter 8

The Debutante in the Woods

Shrode Lake, Alaska, July 2003

The visibility stinks. The roiling gray clouds are spitting rain, the wind makes the little Cessna 185 feel as if it is flying on cobblestones, and the narrow slot through the mountains at Whittier, which is the doorway from Turnagain Arm to Prince William Sound, is shrouded in mist. Katie is in the right seat, up front, sitting next to Kenny Richardson. Kenny is one of the best bush pilots I know. He is leaning forward in his seat, squinting out the front window, keeping us clear of the mountainsides and of other airplanes coming in the opposite direction. While he is concentrating on what's going on around us, Katie is concentrating on keeping her eyes scrunched shut.

She is here because my friend Neil isn't. He's torn his rotator cuff and can't cast his fly rod. I love Alaska and I love Shrode Lake, and would hate having to scrub this trip, but I don't love it enough to be alone in the middle of nowhere. When Katie hears the "Neil's not coming" news, she surprises me.

"I'll go," she says, making me blink.

"Are you sure? It can be cold and wet and rainy."

"If you keep the cabin warm and make sure I get a hot shower at the end of the day, I'll go."

Katie Grace is a Huntington Bay princess, a little girl who waltzed through her perfect childhood, a debutante in a ball gown, who now contends that once outside Greater New York she is camping, and yet she's volunteered to spend time in the remotest of the remote. An A-frame cabin on Prince William Sound. No electricity or indoor plumbing. A creek for running water and a solar shower for bathing. A pillow-top mattress on a canopied bed? Oh no. A sleeping bag. And a canopy? Does mosquito netting count?

Keeping the cabin warm is easy. It's got a fuel-oil stove that has always worked, and I have a shower bag and hanging shower stall that makes life as civilized as can be expected in a cabin with nobody for miles around. Heat water on the stove. Fill the shower bag and hang it from the porch roof support beam over the shower stall. Put her shoes just inside the cabin's door, drape her towel over the doorknob so she can reach it, and make sure her clean clothes are laid out on her bunk. If she's warm, she's not complaining.

***

Bears. Please God, no bears on this trip. In all the years I've been coming to Shrode Lake I've only seen bears twice. Several years ago, one bear in the river about 100 yards below me. Lucky for me the breeze was blowing upstream that day, so the bear couldn't smell me. And one other time. Two bears across a shallow lake just south of the cabin. They lumber off one way, and I hustle off another. Three bears in twenty-three years. Let's keep it that way.

We begin to descend and Shrode Lake, ringed with steep hills, is off the nose. And so is the cabin, maybe 30 yards from the edge of the lake. Kenny is not setting up to land, though. Instead, he slides the 185 to the left and follows Shrode Creek down to where it empties into a salt-water lagoon.

"Let's see if we can spot some Reds," he says. Reds are another name for sockeye salmon. They should be in the creek now, holding just below a waterfall, and from there they return to the small feeder creeks where they were born. They spawn there, and then they die. So we fly the contours of the creek as Kenny looks for fish. He banks the airplane to the right to make it easier for Katie to see the creek out her side, and I hope she is looking that way because two bears are running across a little plateau to the left of us. Black bears, not brown, but to Kate it wouldn't matter.

Casting a fly rod isn't much different from swinging a golf club. Katie's golf swing is smooth and efficient, and that's all it takes to cast a fly rod. I showed her my Montana last fall. Soda Butte Creek in the Lamar Valley, the small channel behind Tim's cabin in Emigrant. She cast a smaller rod and caught rainbows and cutthroats on dry flies. So handling a fly rod with a fish attached to the end of her line isn't new to her, but a salmon, fresh from the salt, at the very beginning of its spawning cycle, is a whole different world. A 3 lb fish is small, a 6 lb fish is average, and some of the males that return to Shrode Creek are well over 6 lb. They are strong, they are fast, and they never quit.

The first afternoon is wet and cold. And it is raining steadily this day on Prince William Sound. There are salmon at the mouth of Shrode, a rock-strewn stream, and flies get snagged in, under, and around rocks. But the fly needs to be near the bottom because that's where the fish are. It seems like Katie's fly snags around rocks on almost every cast. At first, she complains a little. I do too when I sacrifice a fly to the rocky bottom. But as she loses a fly every few casts, her expression of frustration begins to gravitate from mildly exasperated to shades of dark, dark blue. I have heard her imaginative use of F-bombs before, but today's barrage? Wow!

I don't help matters much. Because every time Katie launches into a string of profanities, I ask her to hang on a minute. "I'll help you as soon as I land this fish." I should have simply stopped fishing and helped her, but just as inspiration arrives so does another fish, smashing into my fly.

"Take my rod so that you get the feel of this." This is what I want to say but I never get past "Take my rod…" because she obliterates my good intentions that pave my road to hell.

"Don't you patronize me. I'll catch my own goddamn fish…" And "You asshat." I have no idea what that means. Finally, "You're such a jackass…" A hot shower and several glasses of Côtes du Rhône later softened her attitude a little. But only a little.

***

The rain stops during the night and the early morning sky is a cloudless, almost perfect blue. Katie stands on the cabin's little porch, marvels at the snow-capped peaks surrounding the lake, and says, "You told me this was a beautiful place. Usually, you exaggerate about everything, but you weren't exaggerating about this. It is even more beautiful than I imagined it to be."

We hike back down the river to where Katie's rocks are waiting. The morning's fishing is a sunshiny repeat of yesterday afternoon, except that today her fly slips under a flattish rock, flips up, and wraps itself over and around her fly line. Katie lifts her rod, hoping she's finally connected with a fish. The rock doesn't fight or try to get away. It just lays there. As she winches the boulder to the beach I don't dare laugh.

Instead, I start praying, bargaining with Saint Jude, the patron saint of lost causes. "Come on, buddy. Just one fish. Just one, and if you do that, I promise..." and then her fly line straightens out like a high-tension wire, the rod bucking in her hand. Katie whoops and grabs the fly reel, stopping it from spinning, from letting out line, from letting her fish run. You can't do that. The leader snaps and the fly line goes slack. The salmon, along with another of Katie's flies, takes off for Prince William Sound, the Pacific Ocean, and maybe Siberia.

I lean my fly rod against some blueberry shrubs on the bank; I should have done this yesterday. I stand close enough to help her, but not so close that she can punch me, and after a few rock-free casts Katie hooks a big male. Her hand starts for the reel, but I block her attempt to grab it. Instead, she lets the fish run and allows rod pressure to slow the fish down. With a little more tactfully suggested advice she finally has the fish beaten. It takes at least twenty minutes. Its prominent hooked nose, its kype, tells me it is a male, a great big male.

Katie eases the fish onto the beach, and I pop the fly from the salmon's jaw. When I look up, I see a whole new person.

Kate is beaming, glowing, her competitiveness momentarily sated, enveloped in a happy aura of "It's about goddamn time." A big "I win" grin spreads from ear to ear, almost obscuring the little pearl earrings she refuses to be seen without. She then tells me that we are keeping this fish, that she needs to catch at least one more, and that no, she isn't killing this fish, the next fish, or any other fish she catches. I am. And I do. I show her how to hold this salmon, all 9 lb of it, so that I can take her picture. And my fly rod stays where it is, nestled in the blueberries. A little later Katie catches her second fish with only a few carefully tactful hints from me. I dispatch this fish as well, and these are the only two she keeps. When we get back to the cabin Katie picks a bunch of lupins. They grow everywhere. Some of the lupins go into an empty wine bottle, and some of these flowers serve as a reverential bouquet for her fish. An Irish wake for salmon, I guess.

We arrive home from Alaska on a Thursday. Kate occupies the master bathroom for at least three hours. I am relegated to the guest bath or obscure sections of the landscaping. Katie's two fish go into the freezer, but only for a day, because on Saturday we are having her sisters, Sharon and Wendy, to dinner at the beach. This is why Katie needs to have two fish, and why she festoons them with flowers. These fish belong to my debutante; they are appropriately marked. They have their own corsages.

Katie organizes hors d'oeuvres and dessert and assembles a salad. I am invited to dinner because somebody needs to grill the salmon. She lets me make a sun-dried tomato butter to baste the salmon as it grills, but that is as much as I get to do.

She makes everything else. And at the beach Katie arranges the table and place settings. We always have place settings at the beach, and table linens from Provence. Really. My Debutante is back where she belongs.

Wendy, Katie's youngest sister, her left eyebrow arched, asks, "Did she really catch these fish? Is that the truth?"

"Your sister absolutely caught these fish. She threatened me with celibacy for the rest of my life if I tried to help too much."

"And a one-room cabin without a bathroom? She really spent three days in a one-room cabin without a bathroom?"

I nod yes, of course she did, and tell Wendy, "Every word of this is true."

What else is true is that I was hooked the first time I saw her. Katie's had my number since that December night, that New Year's Eve of 1964, when every dance was a slow dance even when it wasn't. After that first dance, she began to lead every dance we danced together that New Year's Eve, and every dance ever since.

Chapter 9

Coyhaique

Magic Waters Lodge, February 2020

Before my first trip to Aysen in Chilean Patagonia in pre-pandemic 2020, I was convinced that this was an adventure to be experienced just once. See it this one time, and then move on to what I usually do. I usually go to Montana. Usually twice. Usually the same places. Usually the same faces. Safe, known, familiar. And then, on this first trip to Chile, I stared out the airplane's window as it flew from Santiago, south by southeast for two hours, to a little airport in a little town, Balmaceda. The view from the window of the Airbus was one of a vast north–south plain flanked on either side by snow-capped mountains. They reminded me of old gauchos with white hair. The mountains on my right arose between the Plano and the Pacific Ocean. The mountains on the left separated Chilean Patagonia from Argentina.

Tomas Andres Bravo Ampuero, from Magic Waters Lodge, picked me up in front of a terminal that was not much bigger than a large 7-Eleven, and we headed away from the airport, south by west, to a deep valley between small but steep mountains. The mountains were covered for the most part in trees and brush. But some of them had granite faces chiseled by receding glaciers from centuries ago, now scrubbed clean and shiny by wind off the Pacific which drove fat raindrops that scoured the rock of growth. Perched on a little hill just above the valley floor sat the lodge, and in front of it a reed-edged lagoon flashed sunlight back at me. Tomas would be my guide on my first day of fishing tomorrow.

For miles and miles, we had seen small farms and ranches, maybe a car or two, but very few people, who were either walking or on horseback. But regardless of whether they were walking or on horses, everybody had a dog or two tagging along. I wondered if the dogs outnumbered the people here, and if I hadn't arrived on an airplane and hadn't seen telephone and power lines strung along the roadsides, I would have wondered what century I was in.

My friend Les Tugaw, a pilot from Western, was already at the lodge. And so was everyone else that was supposed to be there. Sixteen guests in all, and by the time I arrived, happy hour was in full swing. But I needed a shower before I wandered into the company of other people, so I unpacked, showered, and changed my clothes. I had been traveling for almost thirty hours. I knew I didn't smell too fresh. A Vietnam lesson, once learned and never forgotten, about never wanting to be dirty again.

What did I remember about that first night? I think we had salmon for dinner. I think I had two, or maybe three, glasses of a Chilean Malbec that was amazing. I think I skipped dessert. I absolutely remember Ollie and Hans. Ollie was a very funny smart-ass, a dentist from Colorado Springs. Hans, about my age, was Ollie's father. And later I learned that Hans's father was a U-boat captain during the Second World War. Wow! But

I never ventured past "wow" and Hans never talked about it. And finally, from that first night I knew that there was a guy there, Charlie I think, from Palmer, Alaska, who looked like Santa Claus. I mean, he looked just like Santa Claus, and after being around him for a week I was sure that he came by the big belly and red nose in the usual way one would: beer, lots of beer.

Coffee, first thing, right after showering again and making my bed. I didn't know whether maid service was a daily event here, so I made my bed neatly. Like my mother showed me. Because I just hated climbing into an unmade bed at night, and because the rule growing up was my bed made, my room neat, my dirty clothes in the laundry hamper, my necktie tied correctly, my shoes buffed, my hair combed, and my teeth scrubbed. By now you've figured out that I had to be the first-born child. Parents were always stricter with the oldest child, weren't they? Later I learned that it was much easier to recite "Spectacles, testicles, wallet, and watch," and let that Army grooming mantra cover all bases.

Coffee mug in hand, I stepped out onto the deck in front of the large great room to watch trout break the surface of the lagoon and dine on an early morning hatch of little *Baetis* mayflies. Les and I stood there looking at the lagoon, at the chiseled faces of the mountains surrounding us, the pure blue sky laced with high stratus clouds above us, and the sun behind us, just starting up over the roof of the lodge. And I laughed. I was in trout heaven. Real heaven? Well, real heaven was wherever Katie was. Especially early morning sleepy-head Katie.

***

Tomas, my airport ride from yesterday, ushered us toward a red crew-cab pick-up. We loaded our waders, boots, rods, and reels into the truck bed and climbed in. I intended to ask Tomas about his unusual second middle name, "Bravo." Tomas Andres Bravo Ampuero. Like standing ovation Bravo? Like hooray Bravo? Like encore Bravo?

"Tomas, how did your parents come to give you the second middle name of 'Bravo'? It's a great name. What did you do to deserve it?"

"You see my shape, Franco?" Tomas was built like a fire hydrant. Straight up and down. Solid. And wide. And short. And strong. Smiling, he said, "I was the same shape when I was born as I am now. Just smaller. My mother had a lot of pain getting me born. When my father saw me, and he saw my mother all sweaty and tired he said, 'Bravo.' So, Tomas for my father, Andres for my mother's father, Bravo for effort my mother made pushing me into this world, then Ampuero for my family." He smiled. So did Les and so did I. I liked Tomas right away yesterday when he picked me up at Balmaceda's airport. I liked him even better now.

This first morning in Patagonia, standing several feet back from a meandering little stream, I had to remind myself to slow everything down. So that I could study the water, decide how to fish it, consider the suggestions that Tomas was making as to what fly would work, along with the length and strength of my leader, and to ease the stranglehold I had on my fly rod. Tomas, standing alongside Les, turned to me and asked, "Where are your glasses, Franco?"

"Somebody at the Balmaceda Airport has my Ray Bans, Tomas. I must have left them on the bench when I was digging for my phone. I hope whoever got them needs my Ray Bans more than I do."

"I have an extra pair of glasses in my pack. I'll lend them to you for your stay here."

"Thanks, Tomas. I really appreciate that. I don't imagine there is anywhere close by where I can get some?" I really needed those polarized glasses. To protect my eyes from mis-cast hooks. And to spot fish.

"Not around here, amigo. Amazon. Take at least a week."

"Wow," I said. "We're really in the middle of nowhere."

"Amigo, where we are? This is almost the end of the Earth."

***

The sun was behind me, so I stood back from the edge of the stream because I didn't want to cast a shadow over the water. My shadow could spook a fish. Luckily, I didn't need to squint. The polarized sunglasses Tomas lent me made spotting fish so much easier. This stretch of water was different from any I had ever fished. It was called a "spring creek," which meant that it was fed by springs, and didn't have a lot of structure, like big rocks, to break up the current. Its pace was gentle, so the water tended to meander instead of rush like Montana streams. The bottom was weedy, and the weeds waved almost rhythmically with the slow pace of the water, with channels that cut through the greenery. I wanted to think that the channels were trout highways. Trout cruised them like interstates, but really the trout were everywhere. The weeds were a sanctuary for the browns in this stream. Hooked, they would try to bury themselves in a tangle of leaves, becoming impossible to move. And bugs? Mayflies and caddisflies could fill the air one moment and disappear the next, then come back again a little while later. Cantabria beetles, black claws, long feelers, hard shells, and an inch or two long, regularly fell from trees. The trout went nuts. And then there were dragonflies. Trout love dragonflies. They'd race to get just ahead of a dragonfly, then leap out of the water to catch the dragon in mid-flight. This little stream was like a Michelin-starred restaurant, and the fish ate and ate and ate and ate.

I didn't move for a while because I wanted to absorb all this. So much to see, to consider. I just knelt in the low bushes that camouflaged me and studied the (not very) far bank. Shapes were not distinct in the morning light, but movement was. And I could just make out the gentle tail-swish of a nice trout tucked into and under an overhang of grass across from me. My leader was a 4X, which meant it tapered to a tip that would handle about 5 lb of fish. I tied on a 2-foot length of 5X tippet, which reduced the strength but narrowed the taper of the leader so that it would work with a small fly. I selected a little brown-olive caddisfly imitation from my fly box and tied it to the 5X tippet. A dunk into a bottle of floatant called Flyagra would keep my fly buoyant, and a little of the floatant got rubbed onto the tippet so that everything stayed right on top of the water. Flyagra. To keep the fly floating. To keep the fly "up." And then I just sat there for ten minutes or so, to make sure that the Flyagra soaked into my fly, to make sure that, just like the other "agra," it was going to work.

I've always been in a rush to get on the water, to cast my fly without first looking, studying, planning. Not today. Today was a deep breath day, a go-slow day. I could feel myself spool down. Spool down? That's funny. When I moved the start switches to off on the 767's big engines, they made an unspooling sound, a turbine winding-down sound. Then they stopped, the wheels were chocked, the ground power connected, and the parking brake set. But I was only going as far as slowing down. Slowing and unspooling allowed me to savor, to see, to smell, to feel this stream. To wrap myself in its perfectness and feel my once wounded and now stent-repaired heart slow, because I was in the middle of nowhere, almost to the bottom of South America. I really was in trout heaven.

I made my way slowly upstream, staying back from the bank. I probably wasn't getting into the water very much this morning, but I'm glad I wore my waders because the grass and shrubs that lined this spring creek were soaking wet with dew. I remembered that Tomas said the creek would widen a little further upstream, so I'd probably need to wade then. But right now, I needed to stay hidden, my cast needed to sail high and close to the near bank and my caddisfly imitation needed to land gently. It needed to settle, then be lightly twitched by moving the rod tip. The fly drifted back toward me. Slack was retrieved and my caddisfly was softly lifted off the water. I moved a step or two upstream while making one back-cast and then settled the caddisfly onto the water again. It skittered a little from a wiggle of the rod tip. And a brown trout moved out from under the bank to intercept it. Its head broke the surface, its mouth opened and then closed around my fly.

Tomas was kneeling beside me now with the net in his hands as I, also kneeling, eased the trout to the bank. Then Tomas carefully scooped the fish into his net and held it up for me to see. Fat, golden brown, with yellow and red spots and a pale gold belly. Maybe 19 inches. A really nice fish. High fives, and then Tomas said, "A little small for this creek, Franco."

I laughed and said, "I'll take that all day long, amigo." Tomas dunked the fish back into the water for a minute, then lifted it again so I could remove the barbless hook. I used a forceps to pop it loose, and the fish was never touched by either one of us. Too much handling could cause a fungus on its skin. The brown never left the net, the net was lowered back into the current, turned on its side, and the trout held for a long second before rocketing away. My trout were always released unharmed.

I checked my tippet for nicks, or wind knots that came from sloppy casting. I'm not a sloppy caster but I checked anyway. I reeled my fly line back onto my reel, secured the fly in the little wire hook-keeper just above the rod handle, leaned the rod against a bush, and lay on my back looking up at the sky. The sun was higher now, and a few clouds ambled by. I could hear Katie interrupting my daydream by asking me why I checked the tippet. She's as methodical as I am but has no patience for my version of careful. Her version zooms along like "Rocket Man." Mine plods along like "Lazy Mary get out of bed, get out of bed, you gotta get up in the morning." A song my Nana Clara sang to me when I was Little Frankie.

"You just made that same baguette recipe two days ago. The same one you always make. Why do you need to look at the recipe again?" Katie's challenge dripped sarcasm. I was almost sure she thought I did this to drive her nuts. I really didn't. I've been operating with cockpit checklists, which are like recipes for airplanes, for what seems like forever. I can't help it. But I didn't tell her that. I had to check the tippet. It was part of a ritual, and rituals had to be obeyed. I spoke with her last night, on Facetime, so that I could see her. Maybe that's why she was needling me in this morning's fantasy. Because she stayed in my sleep-dream last night, probably never planned on leaving. I laughed at how, here, laying in damp grass and looking up at the sky, she had nudged aside the burble of the stream and the muted moos of distant cattle and placed herself front and center in this daydream. And I laughed because this was nothing new.

My right hand rested on my aging heart and began to register the beats. My heart, which was not doing very well four years ago, was working so much better now, which is why I came here. Because I was better now. Because I could. Because I really wanted to. Because casting a fly rod has always led me to introspection, to wondering about the whys and hows of the life I've lived. I loved the wondering part.

I picked up my rod and moved back closer to the stream. A few casts placed against the near bank didn't move a fish. I looked to the not-so-far bank and, thank you Tomas's glasses, I made out a shape that moved up and out from beneath overhanging branches, then slid back in the current and ducked under the bank again. And repeated the circuit. I cast my fly to the edge of a foam line of bubbles that paralleled the bank, let it settle and then twitched it once, twice, three times, and paused. The trout's head broke through the foam and ate the fly.

I played the fish and wished my father was here. He would have loved the wild of this place. He's been gone for thirteen years now. The last time he and I fished together was in 1995. In Alaska, for salmon, on Prince William Sound, another middle of nowhere place. We always grilled the first sockeye that my father caught over a wood fire, and he always took a few fish home. Later that year he told me that he wasn't going to be able to go with me anymore. He couldn't. He didn't tell me why, but I saw the slightly dragging left foot and heard the occasional slurred word.

Two weeks before Christmas 2008, a stroke stole most of my father's speech. Two days before Christmas a much bigger stroke destroyed his brain and two days after Christmas his body surrendered. But before it did, I flew to Orlando and drove to Daytona to hold his hand and thank him for taking me with him and Pa, my oh so Irish grandfather, when they went fishing, for making me go to the schools he made me go to, for taking me with him flying when I was 11, for hating that I volunteered to go to Vietnam but always encouraging me while I was there, for coming with me to Alaska and Montana, for showing me, even though he seldom said the words, how much he loved me. I told him all that, and it didn't matter that he couldn't hear me. The words were out there. So, this morning, on this little stream, I wished that my father could have been here and could have been able to see Aysen.

I looked back up at the sky and watched condors soar on thermals.

***

As I moved upstream the brush thinned out, and so did the big trees. Sun now splashed the grass and made the creek flash prisms. Subsurface weeds disappeared into the glare and took the trout with them. They were still there, just harder to pick out. Mother Nature was conspiring to see that my heart relaxed, and I relaxed along with it. The sunlight, the gin-clear creek water, and its dew-soaked, brushy banks made moving quickly almost sinful.

The stream widened just as Tomas said it would, and the scrubby bush along the bank gave way to knee-high grass. There were narrow paths through it that I could follow. I wondered what animal or animals made them. If I were in Alaska or Montana, strolling along on game trails, I'd be singing at the top of my lungs, fondling a canister of bear spray in my hand. In Patagonia the puma occupies the top of the food chain, and they're further east, patrolling open plains, hunting llamas' cousins, guanaco.

Winter storms often change the contours of a river. Nature's way of redecorating, I think. Water from rain and run-off from snowmelt can change the disposition of a river from a gentle presence to a raging intruder in seconds. And over the course of a winter that intruder often overflows its banks and tears trees from their rooted moorings. Some of the trees are hustled downstream by monster volumes of water, and some wedge themselves between and beneath large rocks, stuck fast and unmoving no matter the strength of the current. These serve as a foundation for additional tree stumps and tree trunks and tangles of tree limbs that pile up, causing a diversion in the current, creating a partial blockage of the river's path, creating a snag. Sometimes the fast water scours the river bottom close to the rock-jammed stumps and trunks and tangles of limbs, creating a hole or a trough, and a back-eddy that causes the current to turn back on itself before continuing downstream. The back-eddy is slower as it does a U-turn. Foam and bubbles appear, trapping bugs. And trout take up residence here.

Up in front of me was a snag of several downed trees that had stacked up in the water, close to the bank on the right side of this stream. I was able to see by the shading of the water that there was a deep hole right on its left edge. And there must have been enough mass from submerged stumps to create a beautiful back-eddy, a bug buffet, and there had to be a fish or two dining here this morning.

I didn't get into the water, though. As I got closer to the bank, I heard Les and Tomas talking. I couldn't make out what they were saying but I knew that they were close to the snag and figured that they must be getting ready to fish that eddy. Then I saw Leslie's fly line unfurl and his fly land just above and to the left of the eddy, drift into the foam line, and disappear in a swirl of water, foamy bubbles, and fish. Tomas hollered "Olé!" and Les let out a whoop. Good for Tomas. He was new to guiding. Good for Les. He was new to fly fishing. I sat down on the bank, dangled my feet in the water, and watched grown men turn into boys.

The fish was landed and released, the water calmed, gently turned in its counterclockwise whorl, and then slid by the submerged stumps and the visible branches of the big snag. The bank behind it was lined with small, white flowered trees that reminded me of dogwoods. There were birds all over the surface of the creek, kingfishers, blue with white breasts and red crests, skimming low as they picked insects off the water. Sometimes their wingtips creased the creek's surface, and the birds left a little wake, like airborne speedboats. Tomas pointed them out, identifying them as martin pescadores, when we first arrived at the creek. As I watched, more than a few fish broke the water's surface. Barely a dimple as the fish rose, sipped a caddisfly, and then slipped down again to safety. Kingfishers weren't the only birds present. Ospreys were gliding just above the treetops. Trout were what they hunted. Mostly.

Tomas and Les were still upstream from me. And when Tomas turned to look back at where he and Les had just fished, he saw me. I waved and indicated to him, pointing at the water, that I was going to fish the stretch that he and Les had vacated a few minutes ago. Tomas waved back and pointed upstream, the direction he and Les would be heading. Waving and pointing only. Not shouting now.

The quiet made me happy. This place we occupied didn't deserve extraneous noise. There was a reverence that a stream evoked, not something consciously thought of, more a response brought on by the same question I always asked: "How did this come to be?" I knew the physical reason. But for me, I was awestruck by the beauty of this place, by its magic. Nature's creation was stunning.

At the DakBla River, washing the SPAF Jeep, 1970.

With O-1 001534 at Camp Holloway, 1969. Airplane named by crew chief.

Over Laos with Sgt. Michael Buckland, 1970.

Over Laos, 1970. Praying the engine doesn't fail.

Right: Pvt. William Sansom, my childhood friend, 1965 or 1966.

Below: L-R: Phil Phillips, Doug Krout, Frank Doherty & SPAF Jeep, FOB2 compound, Kontum, 1969.

Above: Prince Sihanouk's meeting place with NVA Generals, Cambodia, 1969.

Left: Dad and I, Shrode Lake Alaska with our first salmon taken on fly rods, July 1980.

Baker River, Chilean Patagonia, Magic Waters Lodge, April 2023.

Above: Overlooking the Paloma River, Chilean Patagonia, Magic Waters Lodge, February 2020.

Left: Shrode Lake cabin, July 1982.

Right: Salmon about to be released, Shrode Creek Alaska, July 1985.

Below: On the way to River of Dreams camp on the Blanco River, Chilean Patagonia, April 2022.

Rainbows on the Baker River, Chilean Patagonia, 2023.

Monte Becker (RIP) and I with brown trout on Blanco River, April 2022.

High bridge over the Yellowstone, Montana, September 2017.

Tim Powell and I, Armstrong's Spring Creek, Livingston Montana fall, 2024. Our last afternoon fishing together.

Right: Absaroka Mountains as a backdrop on our last fishing day, September 2024.

Below: Bitterroot River, south of Hamilton Montana, April 2024.

Tim and I and Emigrant Peak, Emigrant Montana, September 2024. Our last evening. I miss my friend.

Above: Sgt. Michael Buckland, January 1970. Kontum Airfield.

Right: Bill Sansom with Gen. Tony Kropp (my Chaminade classmate) at Northport VA Hospital, 2017.

Below: Last month in Vietnam. Camp Holloway ready room, August 1970.

Above left: Shrode Lake Cabin, Alaska, June 1986. L-R: Neil McLellan, Me, Mark Escobedo, my father.

Above right: Dinner at Tim's Emigrant Montana guest cabin with Tim's wife, Judi. September 2024.

Above left: The Boeing Binder, which holds the tying directions for the flies Everett Caryl taught me how to tie. I still have it.

Above right: My father took me to Columbus Ohio in a Lockheed Constellation just like this, spring 1956.

Above: My first jet, Western Airlines, February 1973.

Left: First flight from JFK to Dublin, Delta 767ER Captain, April 2001.

Katie on the Yellowstone, August 2013. Caught and released all 5 species of trout that the river held. Guide told her it was the "Yellowstone Slam." Rainbow, Citthroat, Cutbow, Brown, Whitefish. Never lets me forget it.

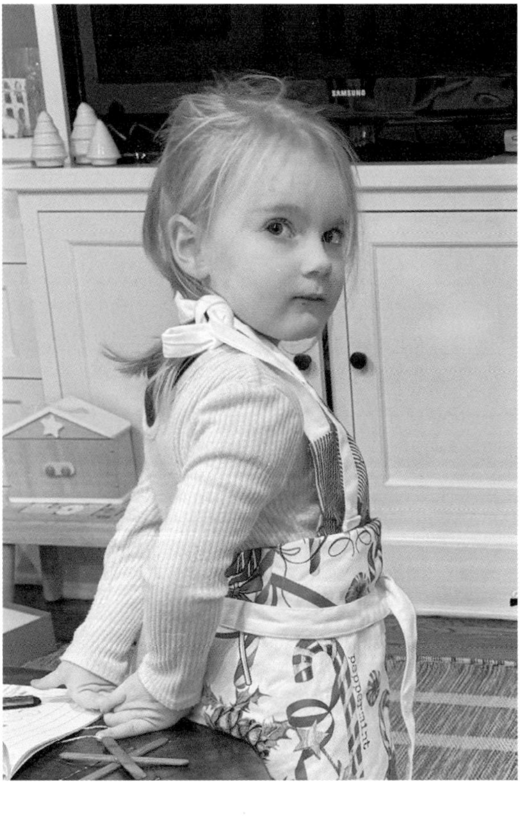

Above left: Katie's Debutante debut, 1966. I have loved her forever.

Above right: Gelato in New Canaan Connecticut, 2024.

Left: Lola, Christmas, 2025.

I tied a medium-sized caddis imitation—olive-brown rabbit-fur abdomen, gray deer-hair wing, dark brown fur thorax—to my leader, took a deep breath, and cast just to my side of the eddy. My rod tip followed the fly as it drifted along the foam, along the edge of the tree branch. I twitched the fly to give it a little movement and to keep it from snagging the branch. And then the fly disappeared in the mouth of a fish. I never saw its head, only its tail. Broad, greenish-brown, and spotted. As I set the hook, I reminded myself to keep the fish out of the snag, otherwise it would break my leader. If the trout made it into the snag, it would be gone. It didn't make it to the snag. I kept it away from the submerged branches, coaxed it to me and my net, landed it, rested it, and got ready to release it. As I tilted my net the trout bolted for the safety of the tangled tree limbs.

***

I leaned my fly rod against a tree and then sat down under it with my back to its trunk. I had no idea what kind of a tree this was. Its leaves were broad but allowed sunlight to slide between them. I could watch and hear the spring creek from here and looking up across the creek the trees opened to reveal an intensely blue sky which made the whiteness of a snow-capped mountain peak, not too far away, dazzle in the sun.

A mayfly landed on my knee. Maybe a *Callibaetis* like the ones I saw in Montana and Idaho and Washington. I dropped my gaze back to the creek and saw dimpled rises. Fish were sipping the hatching mayflies. Occasionally a kingfisher swooped down, intent on catching lunch, its wings the only sound now. But I just watched, content to allow the slowness of the day, the almost total stillness of the late morning to seep into me, to calm me even more.

I leaned my head back against the tree's smooth bark and started to close my eyes. Then stopped and opened them again. Don't doze here, I thought. Take everything in, I thought. I needed to see everything, because I told myself that this would be my only trip here, so I fought the impulse to cat-nap. My hand touched my fly reel. A Hardy Perfect, a reproduction of a reel that was first made in 1891. That would make this type of reel 130 years old. I have been around for seventy-five years. Not nearly as long as the original version of the reel attached to my fly rod. But still, I am more conscious of my age now than I have ever been. I wonder how I made it to 75 years. I wonder how the years went by so fast.

The mountain is backlit by the sun. It makes the snow on the peak look softer. Still mid-morning, still cool, with a soft breeze. My fly rod leans against a branch next to me, and I lean back against this tree and stretch my legs out, and consider time, and days, and how fast they go, and how many are left to me. I hear the kingfishers swoop over the stream, their wings beating ripples on the smooth water which idles slowly off to the side of the main current. I almost feel the air they move as they fly, air that once moved in a hurry past the open window of my little recon airplane. I remember the whistle of air. I lived for the hurry of it past the windows of every airplane I ever flew. My life for almost all my life.

The creek doesn't rush, so the song it sings is more a lullaby. Soft sounds caress me rather than collide with me. I can think about the days remaining. What to do with them. How to arrange them so that they are shared with her. Except for here. Patagonia is not a place for her. And as much as I need her, I need this too.

It seems that days to come are in such a hurry to become days in the past. Some of the days that are in the past take their time leaving. And some of the days that are in the past never leave at all. Dreaming old Vietnam dreams, going backward in time, reminds me of how far and how fast time has come, from that war, to get to now, in this little valley, by this creek. A long way from trying to survive and managing to survive Vietnam until now. A long way from the heartbreak year of Vietnam to the Andes of Chile of now. Time enough to turn a young man into an old one. Time enough now to take a deep breath and remind myself that days to come will certainly pass by too quickly. To remind myself that the days left to me are almost gone.

I run my fingertips over the Hardy reel, its newness celebrating an old design brought back from a century ago. I don't wish that I could be alive that long. That's not something I would ever want. I would rather have stopped time a few decades ago, so that I could be what I once was and act now on the feelings that I have always had when I visualize her freckles and her widow's peak and her ash blond hair and the small of her back and the hollow of her neck and the hazel-gold of her eyes and the smooth perfect curve of her breasts. I cling to the passion I feel towards her and succumb to the riot of need that inflames me because I want her so, that destroys me because wanting her is not enough to overcome the days that have passed and have left me cursed by time. Time that has no compassion for an old man who can't bring himself to surrender to the impotence Time has left in its passage.

***

I proceeded upstream, placing my casts to the front of me and tight to the near bank. Then to the near seam between the slower water and the main current. Then tight to the far bank, flipping my fly line upstream as soon as my fly landed to slow its drift. And as the day warmed, I switched to a fly called a Fat Albert. When Fat Albert landed on the water, it landed with a splat. Which must have resounded like a bell that called the trout to lunch.

Les and Tomas were further upstream from me, and I would have to eventually catch up to them because Tomas was packing our lunch. As I poked through a thicket of *Gunnera*, shrubs with leaves as big as serving platters, I saw Les and Tomas breaking out sandwiches and beer.

"I was just coming to get you, Franco," Tomas said with a laugh. "But Les said he wanted the first pick of the sandwiches." Les had his sandwich halfway to his mouth but stopped.

"Tomas told me to take what I wanted. He said you lost because you were fooling around on the stream and taking too long to get here. See, he's even picked out his own sandwich and grabbed a beer too."

I looked at Les and said, "Ooooooo, I think your pants might be on fire, Leslie."

"How have you been doing, amigo?"

"Not bad, Tomas. Some nice fish. Really nice fish. Mostly 19 to 20 inches or so. Fat. Strong. A good morning, and I'm fine hanging back behind you two. I'll stay within shouting distance." Shouting distance was a figure of speech only. Today was not a day for stray noises in a place that was otherwise quiet. The murmur of the creek, the chatter of birds, the buzz of dragonflies, the splat of beetles as they tumbled into the water, these were enough. Sounds that enchanted rather than invaded, that allowed me to think rather than deflect. And I did. I did think about my life in what was clearly its last chapter. My last chapter. I decided, as I walked along the creek and cast my fly tight to its banks, how I wanted this last chapter to be written.

My words were said aloud now, but the words weren't loud. They barely made a dent in the other sounds all around me, but in saying them aloud I was making a promise to the world all around me. That I intended to do as much as I could, the best way that I could, and when I couldn't do something I would admit that some part of my life had reached its exclamation point, and that I would try to feel completion rather than defeat.

I sent a cast upstream, then stripped in line as the fly drifted back to me. Taking up line so that should a fish eat the fly, the slack in my line was manageable and I could set the hook. A fish ate my fly, and I set the hook. With that the fish shot across the stream and I let some of the fly line that I had retrieved slip through my fingers, keeping just enough tension on the line to maintain control. As the fish came out of the water in a shower of spray, flashing sunlight when it jumped, I could see the soft pinkish-red stripe down its flank. A rainbow, my favorite trout, a fat, 21-inch fish, all streaking speed and indignation. "Yes!" I said to the birds and the bugs and the stream. These were the words, and the days, and the joys, that were meant to fill this chapter of my life. It didn't have to be a long chapter, I decided, but I did need to be sure that this chapter touched on everything that I was able to touch for as many times as I could touch everything.

I sat on the bank with my fly rod across my lap and my feet dangling in the water, and went back to the first thing I decided, that I would accept that bits and pieces of my life could be over, and that I would gracefully admit to myself that I was content labeling "can't do that anymore" with "mission accomplished." And I would be happy with that and accept that and stamp an imaginary "case closed" over that part of my life. I looked up and watched the clouds chase one another across an unbelievably blue sky and laughed out loud. Not a raucous laugh. No. A self-deprecating laugh, an almost embarrassed laugh. I said to the stream and the birds and the bugs and the fish, "Quit trying? Exclamation point? Well, that will never happen." What a lot of crap. The exclamation point will be when I'm not here anymore, when she can't see me anymore, except when she closes her eyes and dreams that familiar fingertips are caressing the inside of her thigh.

***

December 2021: The Blanco, Lago Barroso, and an Old Man on Horseback

There's a slot in the mountains in front of me. The mountains have faces that are sheer slabs of vertical rock. They make the slot look like a hallway. The mountains that make the hallway are smooth, so it appears as if someone has taken a massive cold chisel and cut polished walls of stone. The walls of this hallway funnel the wind that now rips in from the Pacific Ocean, which is not far away. I can watch all this from the great room of the lodge. The mountains are right in front of me, just across a lagoon that I fished just before Covid, which was the first time I came to Chilean Patagonia.

The wind has been blowing since yesterday, when it rained for a short time around nine in the morning, and the wind fired the rain sideways across Lago Barroso. Yesterday I turned my back to the icy raindrops as my friend Ives maneuvered the raft through gusts of wind-driven rain toward the shore. We pulled the raft onto the log skids that served as a dock, tied it down, grabbed our gear, and jumped in the truck. The lodge, two minutes away, was a warmer, dryer place to let this front blow through. Which it did in about an hour. So, Ives and I climbed back into the truck, went back to the lake, re-launched the raft, and it didn't rain again until late last night. But the wind hung around all day yesterday, occasionally blasting across Lago Barroso, and then almost stopping to catch its breath. I timed my casts, waiting out the gusts, waiting for the calm. I was fishing a dry fly, a big dragonfly imitation. They don't cast well in a gale. I waited, and each time the wind eased off, I put my fly into all the little nooks and crannies along the bank. Close to log jams, under branches, into little bays. And sometimes a fish rose to my fly. Ives and I could watch them come to it. Because the water was gin-clear. We could see everything.

This morning, I watch the rain splatter on and hear the wind bounce off the great room's big window. I am not fishing today. It is my last day in Aysen, in Chilean Patagonia. Tomorrow morning, I drive to Balmaceda, then fly to Santiago, then Atlanta, then New York. Almost thirty hours to get home. So, this last day at the lodge I am content to sit by the big fireplace, be warmed by the slowly burning logs, and watch the rain, propelled by the wind, splat against the big window. The sky goes from light gray to charcoal to light gray again as multiple fronts squeeze through the slot between the smooth rock faces of the mountains. The water-saturated clouds spill out over the lagoon and roll above the roof of the lodge, while the wind rattles a window from time to time, as it whistles under the eaves, while the rain splats against the window. It is a noisy morning, but the rain and wind noise is expected, not intrusive. It is the way mornings like this are supposed to be.

The clouds have ragged bottoms, all roiled like water just about to boil. Wisps of gray, tendrils of moisture called virga, dance beneath the slate-colored overcast. They relieve the clouds of their normal flat bottoms, making the sky look like variegated gray pillows all pushed together. Seeing this always makes me wish I had a cockpit wrapped around me, that I was climbing through these clouds, and that I would come shooting out the top of them, all speed, bright sunlight, and smart-ass. Self-absorbed, self-assured, self-satisfied. Soaring with arrogant swagger because I have wings again. But no more. The cockpit has been taken from me because I became too old. I'll never be too old to miss it.

Fish came to my fly yesterday. Not as many as on the Rio Blanco, last week, when I was at the River of Dreams base camp. Ives said the fish in Lago Barroso would be fewer but would be bigger. We were exchanging quantity for size. Who cares? The first fish of the morning smacked my fly, a foam, Antron, and deer hair concoction, an almost Fat Albert, just as the wind began to zip across the lake, just as the rain began to fall, and then the raindrops went racing on the gusts of wind into our faces, and the fish, a fat brown, buried itself beneath a submerged tree branch, and Ives said to pluck my fly line like a guitar string to get the fish to come out of its hiding place. Even though I thought this was pretty cool, the guitar string trick didn't work, the rain was stinging our eyes, the leader broke, the fish was free (it would have been released eventually anyway), so we ran for the lodge. The wind yesterday morning was blowing like an angry freight train.

I called Katie on my phone, Facetimed her and aimed the phone's camera at the slot in the mountains, so that she could see the rain clouds racing through.

"Ha! You're not fishing, are you?" she said with a laugh. "Blown off the water, right?"

"Yeah, but as soon as the rain stops, Ives and I are going back."

"You're nuts, you know that Fah-ran-sis?"

***

We hung around the lodge for an hour, until the wind died off. And when it did Ives and I went back to the lake, relaunched the raft, and motored down to Lago Barroso's far end. Over the edges of weed beds I dropped my fly, let it sit for a moment, then twitched it three times back toward me, and recast the fly to different water along the weeds. The raft slid along on the gusty breeze with Ives using the oars to adjust the raft's angle so that my casts were directed where he wanted my fly to be. I dropped Fat Albert against the bank, above a tangle of submerged branches, above a brown trout that we watched poke its head up, open its mouth, and eat the fly.

Fat, big shouldered, strong. Fighting like all get-out. Ives maneuvered the raft to keep it between us and the log jam. But to the fish, the log jam was home, and that's where it wanted to go. Without taking my eyes off the fish, I asked Ives if we were still using a 4X tippet. We retied the leader after the first fish we hooked broke us off.

"Yes, amigo. Still 4X. I replaced the leader and used 4X. So be careful, Franco. I really want this fish!"

"Me too," I laughed. We could both see that it was a big, chunky brown. And 4X tippet was about 7.5lb test. I hoped that was enough.

Our fish took some time and some finesse. It dove for the log-strewn bottom. It shook its head, swam under the raft, and shook its head some more. All the while trying to get into the log jam. If it did and the tippet rubbed against the submerged branches, we would almost certainly lose this fish. But the raft was maneuvered to keep us away from the tangle of drowned trees, the wind and the rain took a lunch break, and I brought the big brown trout to Ives's net.

"I've got to have a picture, amigo. I've got to have a picture! This is the biggest fish I've ever caught in this lake." I took a picture with my phone of Ives and the fish we caught. Ives' smile was as broad as this brown was long, 25½ inches. We estimated 7½–8lb. A trophy. Then, with the barbless hook removed from its jaw, the brown was eased back into the lake. After a few moments it swam to the log jam and disappeared in the tangle of waterlogged tree branches. Ives was still smiling his Big Fish smile.

"Franco, we have fished the banks of this lake all the way around. And in the last place, my favorite place, you caught a great fish."

"We caught a great fish, Ives. A really, really, beautiful fish. We can call it a day, buddy." And so, we did.

***

I have my back to the fireplace. I can't see it. I don't need to. I hear the firewood snapping as it burns. The big room is warm and comfortable because of it. As I watch the clouds scud along on the wind, I contemplate the week I just spent on the Rio Blanco, north and west of Coyhaique, near Puerto Aysen. The beauty of the river, the dogwood-like trees along its bank, all swathed in white when I first arrived. The fish caught and released, the night sky blazing with stars, the heavens turned upside down because this is South America. And I think about old age. My old age. I can't help it.

When I left the River of Dreams base camp to return to the main lodge, I rode on horseback past the canyon of waterfalls and level five whitewater that made boat and then horseback the only way for people and supplies to get to and from the gauchos' corral to the base camp. And when I arrived back at the trailhead after a week at the camp, I couldn't manage to swing my right leg over the saddle to dismount. After six days of fishing, two hours on Pachuco took all the strength I had. Big rocks, deep mud, steep up and even steeper down, hanging on to the saddle, bracing in the stirrups. By the time we finished the ride I was out of gas. And the humiliation of being unable to get off the horse asked me a question I didn't want to answer. As we rode the van back to Magic Waters, that question poked me all the way to the lodge. "Are you too old now, Frank? Are you too old now? Are you too old?"

***

When did I start drinking tea? I don't know. It seems to me as though I've been drinking it for a while now. I have a cup, steam curling from its surface, balancing on the windowsill. My chair is turned in front of the window so that it faces out, so that on my last day here I can watch the clouds and the rain, whipped by the wind, hustle over the lagoon. Off to the lagoon's left there are four horses grazing, unfazed by the chaos of the weather. They pay no attention to what is going on around them, concentrating on the grass at their feet. They are used to this, I guess. After all, they live here. I watch them and wish I could be as casual as they appear to be. But they remind me of my inability to dismount one of the gaucho's horses two days ago. The notion that my physical ability is diminished bothers me no end.

I look at my hands, at the backs of them. Am I getting freckles from the sun? Well, that's ridiculous. I slather my skin with sunscreen so that the backs of my hands don't get "freckle" freckles. Not from the sun anyway. Are the veins there looking ropey? And darker, bluer? I hold them up to look closer at them. The backs of my hands. I think they are. But I can't hold them too close. If I do then they look fuzzy, out of focus. Anything I hold too close becomes out of focus.

"I think my skin is getting thinner." I state this aloud to no one in particular. I am alone here in the great room. "It looks thinner," I decide, aloud again. I don't really need to talk out loud. But I do. Hearing my own voice is reassuring. I can hear me, which means I'm still here. I wave my hand in front of my face. Yep. Freckles to go with ropey blue veins. Then I look up, see my reflection in the glass of the window. Not puzzled or disappointed in the face I see looking back at me. Just surprised at, in this little moment, how old it appears to be. My face.

"Stand up straight, old man," Katie says all the time. She is not commenting on my posture alone. More a comment directed at my attitude as much as anything else. I make sure I sit up straight in this chair, in front of the big window and my cup of tea. At home if she walks by and sees me slouching, she is sure to comment. And once she starts commenting, her comments become a constant that can envelope the whole day. I tell her sometimes that I never knew how much I didn't know until she came back from long ago to enlighten me. I tell her that I have no idea how I found my way across the North Atlantic at night, but somehow, I managed. It doesn't do a lick of good. "Stand up straight."

How long have I loved her? I think maybe I fell in love with her when she marched up to me and introduced herself, on New Year's Eve, more than fifty years ago, when every dance was a slow dance even if it wasn't, because I didn't want to let her go, because she was all that I could see. "Hi. I'm Katie Grace. Who are you?" I fell in love with her before I knew what it meant to be in love. Before I knew how to love. And because I was an idiot, three decades passed before I saw her again, walking across Grand Central Station. I looked at her and at this moment she was more beautiful than she was all those years ago. I put my arms around her and asked her if she was married and she said she was almost not married and I said, "Me too," and then I kissed her. Now, twenty years later, her "stand up straight" is both a poke in my ribs and a kiss on my cheek.

***

My face is mirrored in the window, and I look at two ears reflected in the glass. They're on either side of my head. I've been noticing them for a while now. Checking on them from time to time. Not so much to see how they are doing. They're doing fine. They must be, because they are still there, and they are still growing. Ironic, my ears, they grow longer while I grow shorter. I used to be 5 feet and almost 10 inches tall. I have a photograph from twenty years ago in which I am looking down at Katie. These days we stand eye to eye.

"Look out the window," my reflection suggests. I do, and my reflection smiles as I look from the window back at an old face, grinning at me. The scene framed by the window is of trees, of horses, of a lagoon and the hallway of mountains. "Close your eyes," the old face says. "Tell me what you see." I do. I close my eyes. But I am quiet. My reflection interrupts my silence. "You see the edge of you, don't you. You see beyond the edge too, out, and out, and out. Beyond the lagoon and the horses and the mountains. An unending vista of nothing."

I know what my reflection is showing me. This edge, when I look out, is like a cliff that drops off into nothing, and when I look up and then out, I can't find the horizon. There is always a horizon. Except not now. It is as if I am looking out at nowhere. And nowhere gets closer every day.

Maybe that's why I am melancholy. Not listless. Just softened. A sense of urgency, yes. But not of desperation. More a recognition of need. A need to structure time, to mold minutes into a carefully choreographed collection of future weeks because, and the reflection in the window knows this, my heart feels funny. My heart is ticking, and for now it's okay, so I don't want to waste minutes thinking about what hasn't yet happened, even though it could. I have other plans. I don't need to talk about old hearts now. I reel my vista back in, away from the edge, and consider the space between me and it. What I can fit into this space. And who should be in it.

I need time for rivers. For the Big Blackfoot and the Bitterroot and the Yellowstone in Montana, the Baker and

Blanco and Paloma and the Simpson here in Patagonia. I will come back to all of these, but I need time for my children and for my grandchildren. And more than anything else, I need time for Katie, the girl who used to live at the top of Richard Lane, the girl I tried to rush into a life for which she was not ready. That was a long time ago. When I was so selfish, when I was so thoughtless. When I never asked her what she wanted, when I thought that what I wanted came first and she just tagged along. When I was so wrong.

There are places I need to revisit. But only with her, because I don't want to be without her for too long. Three or four places we've been to before but need to go back to because we just do. And there, again as before, I need to hold her. And in the last place, in Paris maybe, on a fall afternoon, for perhaps the last time, unbutton her buttons, and kiss the freckles sprinkled across her shoulders, kiss her from the nape of her neck to the small of her back. Kiss her as if it is the first time.

Baker Lodge, April 2023: The Last New River an Old Man Will Probably Ever See

The Baker River roars out of Lago Bertrand, racing south and west for over 100 miles before meeting the Pacific Ocean. On the days that I fish it, I decide that the Baker, Chile's biggest river by volume of water, doesn't lend itself to contemplation. The drifts along its boulder-strewn banks are quick, almost hectic. The opportunity to cast to fish that I could see makes a day on this river an exercise in concentration. Different from the spring creeks near the Magic Waters lodge. On those creeks I can dangle my feet in the water, lean back against a tree and think about my life in what I perceive as its final chapters. Different from the Blanco River, with its little bays and overhanging branches, moving more slowly in many more places than the impatient Baker.

I leave the Blanco River base camp on Friday. I have been here a week and, after fishing all morning, climb on the horse that Jorge brings for me, and ride off behind him and three pack horses for his corral on the other side of the waterfall. The waterfall is the reason I have to ride this horse. Because there is no road, and the waterfall makes the river above it unreachable any other way. The rocky trail is steep, narrow, slippery, and wet. Thank God the horse knows what he's doing because I don't. Two hours later we can see the corral. Jorge can see it, I can see it, and the horses can see it. They pick up the pace. And my back is now complaining bitterly. I climb-dive-fall off the horse, retrieve my duffle, load it into the back of Luciano the manager in training's pick-up, and drive through Coyhaique, a city of 70,000 with no buildings over two stories, to Magic Waters. I haul my duffle to my room, take a long shower, then head for the dining room and the open bottle of Malbec.

The next morning, I drive with Consuelo, Eduardo the lodge owner's wife, to the Baker River Lodge on a gravel road that winds its way through the Cerro Castillo (Castle Hill) National Park, along Lago Carrera, to Puerto Tranquillo, where we stop for lunch. My sea bass came with enough potatoes to feed all the people in this little restaurant. My gringo-ness sticks out like the sorest of thumbs. But I'm with Consuelo, and the owners of the restaurant know her. Everyone is gracious, which doesn't surprise me. Chile is a gracious, smiling country.

The road through Cerro Castillo borders a preserve for huemules, a small, protected deer. If I see one, Consuelo warns me, I have to tell her, because they are very rare. And as we crest a small hill there is Consuelo's deer, walking nonchalantly along the edge of the road. She slows to almost stopping, her voice musical in her excitement. The huemul is unfazed; Consuelo's face is graced by the most beautiful of smiles. As I said, Chile is a smiling country. Finally, after five hours, we are at the lodge. I drop my duffle in my room, put on my waders, string up my rod, and meet Luciano, one of the guides. For an hour or two we'll be chasing rainbows.

The Baker is wide, much wider than the Blanco or the Paloma, its color grayish from glacial run-off. A grayish tint that nonetheless flashes prisms as it hurries past me. A river that announces trout. I can see them gliding across the current, just above the rock-strewn rapids, rising to sip small flies that somehow float on the surface, despite the river's speed.

Lucy is in our raft. She is small, part Golden Retriever, part somebody else. Gentle, loving, she belongs to Luciano, who rescued her. Right now, Lucy is standing next to me, her head in my lap, her ears flapping in the breeze as we motor upriver, watching everything that is happening. Happy to be with Luciano, happy to be with me too. Lucy doesn't flinch when a fish strikes, then jumps. A beautiful rainbow has taken my fly, a small imitation of the equally small mayflies that are hatching. She becomes animated as Luciano extends the long-handled net toward the fish and scoops it into the net, and then pops the barbless hook from its mouth. I wonder if Lucy wants to play with the trout because she barks a lot as Luciano releases the rainbow back into the river. As I inspect my fly, my leader, and my tippet, I look at the glacier-capped mountains that soar above the Baker, at Lucy and at Luciano, and decide that all this is what makes days perfect. Today is a perfect day.

When I look at the Baker, I realize that I have probably seen all the new rivers I will ever see. The speed at which it moves reminds me of the speed at which the few years remaining to me fly off my life's calendar. This scares me. I look north, up the Baker, to the icy white glacier and think about how this last chapter should be. I wonder if I should leave life to chance. Or should I direct the final act? I can't know until I think about that which scares me. What scares me is the loss of control.

Choreography, a life planned by my parents, by the Army, by the airline, by the airplanes, by my children, by me. Every move calculated, dissected, parsed, weighed, controlled, balanced. Every move. You think too contrived, too regimented, too constrained? Not me. I like knowing that having my ducks in a row means that I have a good chance at success. I know what to do. Now, physical, not cognitive, limitations plague my way to old age.

The lodge, on the edge of the river, faces north, its glass-windowed great room looking straight up the river as it surges southeast. The view upriver from this great room is of that glacier-crowned mountain, its ice cap glistening in the bright sunlight, glistening as the sun glances off it. Its intense brightness helps define the beauty of this place. From the great room I can see this icy peak that reflects the sunrise. It is here that I struggle with a question that has been nagging at me since last summer, in Montana, with Tim, and the questions he deflected. The question that wants to consider the when and how of dying.

I'm not afraid of dying, so long as I just get to die with no complications or entanglements. Go to sleep. Stay asleep. That's what my mother said she was going to do. And she did. I would simply say, "All y'all! Here is all the money I have left. Here are all my fly rods and Hardy reels. First one who learns to drive a five-speed stick-shift gets the Z3." That part doesn't faze me at all. Because it's just stuff, so it's easy. But really, facing the end can't be that easy.

I ask myself if this is the last new river that I'll ever study with clear eyes. Is this the last new river that I'll ever teach myself how to fish? Is this the last new river where my hand gracefully manipulates my fly rod? These are not simple questions, the answers not straightforward. Because they speak to cognition, coordination, comprehension. With dusk overtaking daylight, I acknowledge a birthday that will occur soon. I will have lived for seventy-eight years. Over fifty years since Vietnam. More than twenty years since holding Katie again. I remember telling her how I looked forward to growing old with her. I have grown old. Me, not her.

The acknowledgement of the decades that have passed asks me to consider, without exaggerating, what I am able to do. Can I ride the horse to and from the base camp on the Blanco? Can I walk through brush and tall grass a mile or two so that I can fish the spring creeks? Am I agile enough to balance standing in the bow of the raft while casting to fish? Is my heart ever going to be strong again? Is my brain okay or will I suffer the same fate as my father? Multiple strokes that eventually killed him—is that waiting for me too?

I am not afraid to die, but I can't imagine losing control of me. I refuse to sit drooling in a corner. And a diaper? I cannot imagine anything more degrading. So I guess I've figured out what I want. To call the shots. To know when to say that I can't do this anymore. And to know that those words will come from me only after I decide when life is too frustrating, or too clumsy, or too sad. Because the deciding factor in all of this is that I am not an anchor. Not to Katie, or my children. Not to anyone. I want to leave on my own terms. With as many parts of me as intact as possible.

What else? Courage, I think. Yeah, courage. The courage to know when to say when. The courage to talk to Katie about this, to ask Katie to see my decision the way that I see it, and for her to say to me that it's okay to be done, and to give me a last kiss. That would be the hardest of all. That excruciatingly painful, heartbreaking, magical, eternal, last kiss. Then saying to her that I have loved her forever. So that when Katie closes her eyes and feels familiar fingertips caressing the inside of her thigh, these are the forever words that accompany my fingertips:

"It has always been you, Katie Grace. It has always been you."

Chapter 10

Explaining Anything to Francis Aloysius...

Lloyd Harbor, Fall 1959

Author's note: When you read the dialogue, the words spoken by the elder O'Dochartaigh must be said aloud using the best Irish accent you can muster. It's important that this be done in the song of my grandfather's voice. You need to sound like him (and every nun from Ireland who has ever aimed an eraser at me). I'll italicize the Irish accent parts, so you'll know when to give them the best "Oh Danny Boy" you've got.

My father, Francis John, was someone who, as a kid, could start out for a movie theater with a dime in his pocket. The price of admission may have been twenty cents, but he was always sure he'd find the extra dime somewhere along the way. Happened his whole life. Drove me nuts. The only person one step ahead of my father was his father. Always one step, one wry observation, one skeptical "*Ah, sure now,*" ahead. Drove my father nuts.

For example, consider this. Before the war my father was pushing racks of clothes in the Garment District in New York City, between 7th and 8th Avenue, from 34th Street to 40th Street. That was his life. And then the Japanese attacked Pearl Harbor and Dad enlisted as an Aviation Cadet in the Army Air Corps. I asked him, years ago, why the Army Air Corps, and he said he just wanted to fly an airplane. No rallying to the drums and the flags and the bugles. He just wanted to fly an airplane.

A high school education, not quite 22 years old, and somehow now a lieutenant, with silver wings on his chest and a B-24 to plow through the air with. Lacking any mechanical aptitude whatsoever. Needing malpractice insurance before touching any kind of tool. My father. A pilot. In a B-24. Loaded with bombs. Jesus, Mary, and Holy Saint Joseph. "*Ah, sure now,*" said my grandfather.

Surviving the war. That's like finding the extra dime, right? More like finding the leprechaun's pot of gold if you ask me. The B-24 was as nimble as an airborne shoebox, and there were Japanese Zeros to contend with almost every day, but Francis John survived. And one of the pilots in his unit, who flew for TWA before the war, promised my father a job flying for the airline if he wanted it. If he wanted to keep flying rather than push racks of clothes in the Garment District. Not much of a decision there. Only one problem. There's always one problem. The driver. Who? The driver. You know, the servant. My grandfather was convinced that my father had a servant. And as far as he was concerned that was reason enough to stay put. Did Francis John have a servant? Not exactly. But nothing much Francis John said could convince Francis Aloysius.

Dad was hired by Trans World Airlines on August 6, 1945, six days before his twenty-sixth birthday, number 754 on the pilot seniority list. Not bad for a kid from Hollis (part of New York City's borough of Queens), the only son of Irish immigrants. A big deal really. And believe me, Dad was very aware of his early climb up the ladder of success. Garment rack pusher to aviation cadet to lieutenant to B-24 pilot to Army Air Corps captain to airline pilot. "*Fair play to you,*" my grandfather would say. And he did say that, but not right away.

Because my grandfather loved the idea of my father's uniform and his rank of captain, and his occupation as a pilot, with no connection whatsoever to the "*Goddam Brits.*" (Age-old animosities existed even when separated by the Atlantic Ocean.) Now came the hard part. My father was going to have to explain to my grandfather why he was planning on resigning his commission and leaving the Army for a job in an industry my grandfather knew next to nothing about.

"So, Da, I've been hired by an airline, TWA. I'm going to go to work for them as a pilot. I've resigned from the Army and will start training in Kansas City in a few weeks. Think I'll probably start on a Martin 404 freighter and be stationed in Chicago." Dad said that his father looked at him for a long minute, then shook his head ruefully back and forth and began a rejoinder that was so animated that my father didn't think he was going to be able to get a word in edgewise.

"*Why would anyone want to give up a job where he's an officer with a fine uniform and an airplane to fly. Ah, yez can't convince me that whatever you'll be doin' will be better than what yer doin'. You're an officer with a fine uniform and ya get ta have a great big aeroplane ta go around in whenever and wherever ya want. And ya have a servant, don't ya now.*"

Dad said he had to think about that last bit. About the servant. So he looked at my grandfather and said, "Servant? I don't have a servant, Da."

My grandfather looked back at him with a "*got ya now*" smile and replied, "*Ah sure but ya do. The man that comes and takes yez ta work and when you lot are done, he takes yez home. A man who comes to take yez to work and then comes to take yez back is a servant. Ya have a servant, so.*"

My father didn't dare laugh. At least not yet. But he did smile, he said. He couldn't help it. "No, Da. He's not a servant. The sergeant who comes to take me and the crew to the airplane is a driver, not a servant. He's a driver who takes us all to and from the flightline. Every flight crew has one. And sometimes several crews are loaded into one big transport truck and taken to the flightline. And whoever is driving us is exactly that, a driver."

"*Ah Jaysus,*" my grandfather shot back. "*Ya don't understand. A man comes and takes ya to work, and when yer done he takes ya home. That's a servant. Ya has a servant, and I can't understand why you'd give up a job like that!*"

Eventually Francis Aloysius came around. But only eventually, and grudgingly. Because giving up was giving in and giving in was surrendering, and surrendering was admitting he was wrong. And Francis Aloysius seldom admitted to being wrong about anything.

To me this story was very funny. Because my grandfather's preoccupation with the "servant" exposed his determination to climb another rung on the ladder of respectability. Because it wasn't too long ago that "No Irish Need Apply" signs hung in the windows of many places of business. And because, being a true son of the "*Auld Sod,*" he clutched tightly to grudges, especially old grudges. Thus the "*Goddam Brits.*" And funnier still was that he never admitted to being wrong. Ever. Best of all, though, it was so clear to me that my father's acorn didn't drop but a few inches from his father's tree.

And me? My acorn? Well, I could tell you that I am more reasonable than either one of that lot. That I am gracious when mistaken, and quick to apologize without a hint of sarcasm or insincerity. So, my acorn landed a good half mile from my father's tree. Easily a good half mile. You know I'm right.

"*Ah, sure now, young Frankie, and fair play to you.*"

Chapter 11

Mr. Scudder's Houseboat

Lloyd Harbor, Spring 1954

We weren't going the way we usually went. We always headed to the South Shore, to the Great South Bay. My father rented a skiff and small outboard engine that always took us to the channels near the Captree Bridge. Porgies schooled up near the bridge's upright pillars, fluke wallowed on the sandy bottom there, and small, toothy blues cruised the channels beneath the bridge, gorging on the pods of baitfish that tried but couldn't get away. And when the blues started chopping their way through the baitfish, gulls whirled overhead and dove into the water, grabbing the remains that floated to the bay's roiled surface. We weren't going there today. And there was one more thing that was different. My grandfather, Pa, wasn't with us.

Our station wagon was aimed north. The Great South Bay was the other way. So was Pa. I looked out of my window for a little while, and then looked at my father, who hadn't said a word yet.

"This isn't the way. And where is Pa? Where are we going?"

"You're right. Not the way. We're going to the North Shore. There's a harbor I thought we'd try. I didn't bring Pa with us this morning. I'll tell you why later. First, we're going to stop in a town close by to where we'll get a boat. We need to get some breakfast."

"Donuts and beer, or a real breakfast? Like pancakes? And I didn't tell Mom about the beer. I swear. I don't know how she found out."

"Not donuts and beer. We can't buy beer anyway. Not until lunchtime. It's called a blue law. Sundays only."

Dad drove down a big, twisty hill, past a little round white building that said "Laurel Hollow Police" on a sign over its door, then past a pretty white church perched on the bank of a pond, then a place that said "Cold Spring Harbor Fish Hatchery," then past King Neptune's Clam Shack and a boat launch and some fancy old houses, then down another hill and into a town with a stoplight on its first corner. And he finally did stop in front of a store that said "Richter's Bakery."

"Come on, boyo," Dad said, mimicking Pa. In we went. And it smelled so good! Two bagels with cream cheese, two slabs of crumb cake, a jug of orange juice, a white bag, and a reminder to tell Mom I had orange juice. Not Guinness.

Back in the car, we went one block before turning north. Dad said, "We'll be at the harbor soon, and get the boat."

"What harbor?" I asked.

"Huntington Harbor. We're going to Isaac's boat launch. He's got a rowboat and outboard set aside for us. And bait. We'll go looking for flounder."

Lars Isaac was a stump of a man with a fuzzy white beard, wearing a battered knit hat and an old black turtleneck sweater. He was standing on an ancient dock built out over the water, next to a rowboat that looked as battered as his old hat. Dad looked at me, then at the boat, then back at me, and assured me that the boat would be fine, then told me that I needed to remember to tell Mom that the boat was perfect, just like the orange juice. We loaded our fishing rods and a cooler that now held the bagels and the crumb cake and the juice and a cardboard container full of sandworms. When Dad put the sandworms in the cooler with breakfast, I thought, "Gee. If the worms get hungry, I hope they eat Dad's bagel. Not mine." And then I realized how silly that was. If the worms started in on his breakfast, he'd take mine and give me their leftovers. Then look at me and laugh. Everything of mine was his. He always pulled tricks on me like that until the day he died.

My father let me bring the skiff out of Huntington Harbor, swing around the lighthouse that guarded its entrance, and turn west into a different harbor. Wide at its mouth, the harbor narrowed as it stretched west. I slowed the boat and Dad stood up, then knelt one knee on the small wedge seat snugged in the bow while gripping the gunwale and scanned the bright green eelgrass along the harbor's tree-crowded banks.

"Okay. Chop the power." Airplane talk, but I understood, and the skiff slowed and then almost stopped. The incoming tide took over, gradually pushing us further into whatever this harbor was called. Then my dad quietly and gently and slowly eased the anchor into the water. No throwing, no splash, no noise, no spooked fish. Pa would approve. That's what his "and fair play to you" meant. I didn't pay attention to everything, but I paid attention to things like this. We rigged up with small lead sinkers and long-shanked hooks, and threaded the sandworms onto the hooks, and the sandworms, which had fang-like pincers for mouths, tried to bite my fingers. I flipped my line towards the eelgrass, trying not to make a big splash or a lot of noise, and as the sinker hurried toward the muddy bottom, I looked east from where we came, and west down to the harbor's end, then to the south bank, and finally the north bank. I had no idea where we were.

Trees grew everywhere. Maples and oaks and dogwoods just beginning to push out buds. I knew their names because Dad and Pa both told me their names. The west end of this harbor narrowed to more eelgrass and to what had to be a marsh. And there was a road just beyond the marsh because I could see cars go by. Not a lot, just every now and then. Off to my right, on the north bank, were more trees, and right on the high-tide line was a double-ended houseboat, raised up off the sand by vee-shaped supports. There was a ladder at its stern so whoever lived there could climb on board, and the houseboat even had a crooked little metal chimney poking out of its roof. Somebody must live there.

Doink, *doink*, *doink*. Little taps. Little nudges. Barely perceptible. Somebody's down there, fooling around with my sandworm. I sat still. Then a slight tug. I sat even more still. And another, more determined tug. I lifted my rod tip. Flounder. Another more definite lift set the hook. Three or four more like this and we'd have dinner. As I reached for the landing net, I saw Dad's rod bent over too, so I deposited my fish on the floorboards and handed the net to my father. The pointy-nosed pliers removed my barbless hook from the flounder's jaw. The fish was at least a pound, so I knew we'd take it home, then looked to see how big my father's fish was. Oh, good. Mine was bigger. Did this really matter? You bet it did!

The "bite" continued for another hour or so and then began to taper off. In another thirty minutes the incoming tide would be fully high, and the fish would stop feeding while the tide turned and began to drop. Dad put his rod up, opened the white bakery bag and retrieved the bagels and the juice. I held my rod in one hand so that I could catch a few more fish than he did, picked up a bagel and inhaled it so that I could get to the crumb cake before he did. Get to the piece that was a little bigger than the other piece. Dad didn't look at me. He picked up the bigger piece, put it on his seat, next to him, and scanned the entrance to this harbor. I started in on the smaller piece of crumb cake but followed his gaze, trying to see what he was straining to see.

A snub-nosed scow chugged toward us, and as it got closer my father began to haul up our mud-covered anchor, then moved to the stern and started the outboard. Dad waved at the man at the scow's tiller, then followed him into the harbor, right to the houseboat. The scow was secured to a mooring buoy, and the man slid over the side into knee-deep water and waded ashore. We beached our rowboat, climbed out, and walked toward the houseboat.

"How are you, Dick? This is my son Frank. Frank, this is Mr. Richard Scudder." I didn't hear the next few words my father said because Mr. Scudder's right hand enveloped my hand and my wrist and my forearm, a hand that was twisted and crooked and mud-creased and salt-crusted. It took a lot of determination to drag my eyes away and look at a wind-burned, faded blue-eyed, ash-white whiskered face that smiled down at me. Mr. Scudder looked maybe 100 years old or maybe forty years old. I had no idea. He was shorter than my father but twice as thick. Not fat. Thick. Like muscles stacked on top of muscles. A neck that disappeared into shoulders as wide as our station wagon, shoulders which rode on a torso as wide as our station wagon, and a torso which rode on legs that barely fit into his hip waders. I was sure that this man could probably pick up our station wagon just for the fun of it.

I watched as Mr. Scudder and my father walked east along the seaweed-strewn high-water mark, both pointing and gesturing at the few buoys that bobbed nearby. I couldn't hear what they were saying, so instead of trying to eavesdrop I turned to look at the houseboat. There was an embankment behind it that rose maybe 15 feet. I could hear cars so there must be a road up there, and I figured it must be part of the road that crossed the marsh at the west end of this harbor. Part-way up the bank was a flat spot that sported an outhouse. I always thought that outhouses had quarter-moon cutouts in their doors. This outhouse didn't. It had a fish. And on the beach, close by the stern of the houseboat, were wooden casks with a pipe leading to them from a rain gutter that surrounded the houseboat's roof. So, no indoor plumbing. Kind of like Boy Scout camp every day.

I walked up to where my dad and Mr. Scudder were standing, and the first word I heard Mr. Scudder say was "boat." Then my father said "boat." "Boat" was a word that meant so much more than just a boat. I heard "money" and "mooring" and the number of months and the use of a dinghy to row out to a moored boat. And of course I went from these words to, "We're gonna get a boat!" And that's as far as I got because Dad aimed me back toward our beat-up skiff. We pushed off the beach, and he let me drive.

From this harbor without a name, we headed back toward Huntington Harbor and Lars Isaac and what I hoped were answers to the nine bazillion questions zooming around inside my head. When we were clear of the buoys and lobster pot markers and steering toward the lighthouse, my mouth formed a question that never made it any further than, "Can…?"

"I'm going to tell you what's going on, but don't interrupt me like you always do. Just let me explain, and after we get to the car and I have finished telling you what I want to tell you, then you can ask questions."

"Can I just ask you one right now?"

"What about?"

"Who is Mr. Scudder?"

"I get to call him 'Dick,' but you always address him as Mister Scudder. He lives in that houseboat and is a clammer. He digs clams and sells them. Those poles in his boat are attached to clam rakes and that funny box you saw stretching out over the left gunwale is called a culling board. It's a grate that lets clams that are too small to keep fall back into the water. But Mr. Scudder doesn't let the seed clams, the little clams, go into the water just anywhere. He puts them back close to his houseboat. He's got a clam farm at his front door. One more thing. His family has been in Lloyd Harbor since before the Revolution. The Scudders fought with George

Washington. The 'Notorious Scudder Brothers.' They rowed across Long Island Sound to Connecticut and smuggled guns and ammunition back to the Continental Army. And the harbor is called Lloyd Harbor."

"What about the boat? Are we getting a boat?"

"I told you that I'd tell you, but right now you need to watch where we're going, boyo."

***

We didn't drive south toward Hicksville. Instead, when we left Isaac's, we continued north along the water. I was looking at the names of the narrow lanes and the names of some of big houses. I didn't know houses had names, but some of these did. We turned onto Mill Road, and then again onto West Neck Road, down a big hill, and then onto the road across the marsh that I had seen from where we were fishing. Dad called this a causeway. To my right, he said, was Lloyd Harbor. The water on the left was Cold Spring Harbor, and I should pay attention because I'd be able to see Mr. Scudder's houseboat as we drove past it. He'd tell me when.

"When." There was the crooked stovepipe, and an ancient pick-up truck that was hidden behind the houseboat. I craned my neck to see as we drove past. A little further and we turned north again onto a gravel road, up a little hill, then up a bigger hill, and down into a small valley of oaks and dogwoods. And when we got in the middle of the valley, Dad stopped.

"Out with you. And pay attention." He gave me a minute to look around. And I did, turning in a complete circle. Dad had turned too, facing east, and pointed to the trees in front of us and said, "This is our family's now. Your mother and I bought this. The oaks and the dogwoods. Maybe 3 acres, and we're going to build a house here. Further along this road is more water, Long Island Sound. There is a beach there where we can swim. Not just ours—it will belong to other families who move here. If we go back the way we came, to Lloyd Harbor, there will be a dock there…"

"Will we keep our boat there?" He looked at me and started to say something but burst out laughing instead.

"I'll teach you how to use it when we get it."

"Does Mom know we're getting a boat?"

"Not yet. And you aren't going to be the one to tell her either. I will. Spill the beans, boyo, and this is as close as you'll ever get to that boat."

"You still don't believe me about the Guinness, do you?"

I stood looking at the oaks and the dogwoods, all manner of ideas racing around inside my head. Move! We're going to have to move. To Lloyd Neck. To the water and the woods and Mr. Scudder and a boat. Maybe a BB gun, and maybe I won't have to go to Catholic school. That made me laugh. Of course I would go to Catholic school. I'd probably be going to Catholic school forever. A new school means new friends, and it means I'll probably never see Rainy Walsh again, and that is terrible. My mother says I get all moony over Rainy Walsh. It means I'll never have to sit still in Sister Adelaide's classroom anymore. I know how to duck because of Sister Adelaide. Because she always throws strikes with a blackboard eraser. High cheese. That's what Pa calls fastballs thrown high and inside for strikes. And that's what Sister Adelaide throws. Erasers. For strikes. High cheese ones.

***

The part of Lloyd Neck where we built our house was called Fiddlers Green. It had a private road that ran from Lloyd Harbor to the sound, and the families who built there were pilots from airlines that flew out of Idlewild and LaGuardia. TWA and American and Eastern and Pan American and United. Dads who learned to fly in the Army Air Corps. Parents who knew city blocks and little squares of trees and trolley cars and maybe, depending on how long the bus ride took, Far Rockaway or Coney Island. They knew Queens Boulevard or Arthur Avenue or the Brooklyn Bridge or the Lower East Side or Levittown. Places where houses didn't have names, and trees grew in intervals along sidewalks, and where places full of trees were reserved for Sunday rides. If your family had a car. Antonio DeGuira, Pop Pop, my Italian grandfather, who made ravioli and porchetta, had a car with a rumble seat. Francis Aloysius O'Dochartaigh, Pa, my Irish grandfather, who loved finnan haddie and boiled potatoes, didn't have a car. We had a car. A green '47 Chevy. How else would my father get to Idlewild or LaGuardia?

It was all I could have hoped it would be, this place called Lloyd Neck. Settled before the Revolution. Tree-filled, with rabbits and deer and foxes and pheasants. Water on all four sides, the Neck connected to the mainland by a causeway built over a marsh. And in the fall the eelgrass in the marsh turned gold and the oak leaves, now spent from summer, turned gold too. Not to be outdone, the maples and dogwood blazed red. The days grew cool, and every year October decorated the banks of Lloyd Harbor in a kaleidoscope of color.

Our boat was a small runabout. An Old Town, made in Maine, with an Evinrude outboard. Big enough for my father, Pa, and me to fish from. Big enough to pull a water skier, and as promised, just the right size for an 11-year-old boy to drive. He kept the promise he made me, my father. But there were boat rules. Dad had rules for everything, and now for this boat. Breaking any of them meant no boat driving for me. So, I didn't break any boat rules because driving the boat was so cool. Especially for an 11-year-old boy.

We kept the Old Town with Mr. Scudder for the first two years we had it. There was a dinghy tied to one of his houseboat's pilings which Dad used to row out to our boat. He'd load the dinghy with me, Pa, our fishing rods, crumb cake, and Guinness, and off we'd go. But if I got to bring the boat around to the beach on Long Island Sound by myself, I never used the dinghy. I swam out, untied the boat, and swam back to the beach in front of the houseboat, towing the boat by its mooring line. And if Mr. Scudder was there, I had the chance to talk to him.

"You can call me 'Dick' if you'd like, young Frank. It's okay by me."

"Thanks, but I better not. Dad told me to call you Mr. Scudder, and I think I should stick to that. If I make a mistake and my father hears me, he's not going to be happy. I don't want anything to go wrong so that I'm not allowed to drive our boat."

Another rule. No personal questions. Both Mom and Dad explained the difference between a sort of everyday question and a personal one. An everyday question could be wanting to know how long it took a clam to grow, how Mr. Scudder raked clams at high tide, when the water was much deeper. Where were the clams sold? A personal question would be if Mr. Scudder had ever been married. If not, how come? If Mr. Scudder wanted me to know things about him, he would tell me, they said. And if he didn't, he wouldn't. So don't ask questions like that. A finger or two was aimed at my nose to emphasize that point.

"So how long does it take for a little clam to be big enough to keep? How long does it take to row across the sound? How big was the boat your great, great-uncles—they were your uncles, right—rowed and how many guns and ammo could their boat hold? Did they do this at night? In the rain? Did they ever have any close calls? Do you still have any of their stuff? Do you wish you could have done that too? Would you? Would you do that too? How come you live by yourself? Oh, no. Wait. I didn't mean to ask you that. I'm not supposed to ask you questions like that. Nuts!"

"Do you know how to splice a rope? The end of a rope? To keep it from fraying? Let me show you."

And with that Mr. Scudder handed me a rope with raveling ends. It wasn't spliced, we began splicing lessons, and he began to talk. About some of the questions I asked, but for the most part about things he wanted to talk about. And I learned about rope and knots and the lifespan of clams and the kind of clams that lived in Lloyd Harbor and when to harvest them. And:

"Pink sky at night, sailor's delight; pink sky at dawning, sailor take warning." And if the wind is strong out of the east, be sure to have a rain slicker with me. Mr. Scudder said I needed to develop a weather eye. I had to think about that for a while, and after all these years I'm still not sure what a weather eye is.

Our boat was moved to Fiddlers Green harbor frontage when the village of Lloyd Harbor approved dock and mooring plans. Dad wanted a good spot, so we moved the boat as soon as we could. But that didn't mean that I didn't spend time sitting on the ladder leading up to Mr. Scudder's houseboat. The visits weren't as frequent as I would have liked. I mean, he did work according to the tides, digging clams and maintaining his "farm," and I did go to school. But I always looked out the school bus window as it passed the houseboat. I even bought a leaky old rowboat, a small outboard, a clam rake and culling board, and two metal bushel baskets. And I became a waterman, at least for two summers, from the end of my sophomore year until the end of my senior year at Chaminade. Digging clams and talking to my friend. But only for the first of the two summers.

The smoke stopped curling from the crooked chimney in mid-May, in 1962, just before the end of my junior year. For a while I thought nothing of it. It was getting warmer. Maybe Mr. Scudder had stopped firing up his woodstove. But on a brief spell of chilly weather no wood smoke curled up from the chimney either. So, on a Saturday morning I rode my bike to the harbor and walked from where our dock was, along the high-tide line, to the houseboat. His scow bobbed on its mooring line. It sat low in the water, almost to the gunwales, slightly listing. Full from the last rainstorm, I guessed. That shouldn't have been. And the rain barrels were full. No one had used the water in them. And for the first time ever, when I called his name and then called it again, no one answered. And I knew.

I asked at Top C, the shack in Huntington Harbor where I sold my clams, about Mr. Scudder. There would not be a service, I was told. He had no family. No one to mourn him or celebrate him. I didn't know that until now, because of course I didn't ask him, and he didn't offer. His was my first experience with death, with loss, with unanswered questions and blank spaces where answers should have gone. Mr. Scudder's words would stay with me, and his smile would remain clear in my memory, but my weather eye? I still have no clue.

I went back to the houseboat a few more times. And then it was gone. And the scow was gone. But every time I passed by where the houseboat used to be, I looked. I knew it wasn't there. I looked anyway. I knew his houseboat was gone. Oaks and maples had begun to grow where it used to be. Their leaves would turn gold and red and beautiful in the fall.

Chapter 12

The Boeing Binder

New Canaan, Connecticut, Spring 2024

My finger runs down the side of an old three-ring binder that once held the operating manual for a Boeing 737-300. That airplane, explained in this manual? Well, there may be a few still operating in faraway places without rules that are too strict with regard to an airplane's age or condition. But for the most part, the old 737s that still exist languish in some desert boneyard, already cannibalized and waiting to be turned to scrap. I look at the binder, smile sadly, and tell myself that most of these old Boeings don't fly anymore, and the old pilot that used to fly them doesn't fly anymore either. The pages of this manual have been gone for almost forty years, which is about how old I was then, when I replaced the outdated pages of the manual with notes, carefully printed on graph paper, in blue ink, explaining and diagramming the construction of flies. Not flying flies. Fly-fishing flies.

In 1985 I traded beaches for rivers, sunshine for snow, and surfboards for fly-rods. A better than even exchange, I was sure. The loud Pacific and Venice's crowded beach for a river I often had all to myself. Rivers, especially rivers in the panhandle of Idaho, were solitary places. Which was perfect as far as I was concerned. I needed a place that would allow me to hide from the gunfire that banged away nightly in the horror show of my dreams. I picked up a fly-rod, and it helped me keep the horror show away.

I moved our family from a tiny bungalow on the ocean side of Lincoln Boulevard in Venice to a three-story Victorian that overlooked Spokane from the South Hill's Canon Hill Park. The Venice bungalow could easily fit in the garage of the Spokane house, my two little girls could walk across the park to Cataldo Catholic school, I could commute to Delta's hub in Salt Lake to fly my trips, and I could try to lock Vietnam away in a room I never again had to visit.

The fly-fishing patterns in the binder aren't anything special. Just good flies to use to learn from. Because their construction is basic. Building blocks. A Gold-Ribbed Hare's Ear and a Pheasant-Tailed Nymph and a Royal Wulff, and an Elk Hair Caddis, and a Parachute Adams. Classic, famous, and everyday effective. I know the instructions for those flies are saved within the binder, but they aren't only what I think about when I look at the pages. I always think about the man who taught me how to tie them, who became my friend, who never asked me for my advice or my opinion but would let me offer them to him anyway. Who talked about growing old. Who displayed his frustration with that. Who shared some secrets with me and opened his heart to me. Without reservation, or filter. Never a filter, my friend, Everett.

But it was our shared time that mattered most. Because that time lent itself to questions and answers that eventually got to the heart of what Everett wanted to talk about. And Everett talked a lot about growing old. About not giving in. Everett refused to give in to time that was rushing by him. As trust in one another got stronger, as friendship became anchored in that trust, questions came in a steady stream from Everett. Not exactly a two-way street. He did most of the asking, and I did most of the answering. But time shared, with a man almost three decades older than I was? Terrific.

There was a place I loved, a long, alkaline lake which was formed by receding glaciers, snugged up against the east side of the Cascades. Lake Lenore, just north of Ellensburg, Washington. It held Lahontan cutthroats, big, strong football-shaped trout that adapted to the alkaline water. The cliffs that ringed the north side of Lenore were glacial till, loose rock of striated colors that danced in the sunlight. The first time Everett showed me this lake thousands of what I thought were seed pods drifted, danced, and twirled in the breeze. Everett said they were really spiders' eggs, secured in stark white strands of web, like wisps of fluff, like airborne nurseries. I fished here often with Everett, on this lake formed centuries ago by flood waters that surged west and south, that carved up the earth, creating valleys between mountains, exposing multi-colored rock and freeing up buried springs that filled the depressions left in the flood's wake.

***

As the years, along with Everett, passed, I thought often about what he decided to do. How brave it was. How daring for that time, in those days, in that community of solid, stolid Swedes and Germans and Norwegians and Scots, who were upright and stoic and rigid and unbending. As the years, along with Everett, passed, I began to understand about the very personal, and sometimes not so private, fight men who were aging waged against aging. As I consider this now, I realize that my first inclination, to laugh, would have been way off base. What Everett did was like being a one-man Charge of the Light Brigade against the Army of Diminished Ability. Against the Army of Flagging Potency. Against the Army of What the Hell Happened to Me. Everett raged against the passage of time, the passage of time that caused physical ability to desert his desire and left his desire to fend for itself. Because his hunger hadn't ebbed. Only his erection.

On another morning, not long after the first time at Lenore, we drove west on Route 2, back to the striated cliffs and the alkaline water and the big trout. Everett was fidgety. Usually, he snoozed. But not this morning. Instead, he looked long at me as I drove and then said, "Gloria came over last night. She always comes over on Monday night. And I couldn't perform. She's a young woman, 66, and expects sex. And I couldn't perform." Jesus, Mary, and Holy Saint Joseph! My fingers clamped down hard on the steering wheel, eyes glued to the road's white center line, concentrating on not running off into a ditch, concentrating even harder on not laughing.

Gloria and Everett were married but didn't live together. She managed an old apartment building in north Spokane, and Everett lived with a menagerie of cats on the west side of the city. Monday nights they spent time together, which until last night culminated in romance. Last night his erection deserted him.

I never questioned any of this. I decided that it just wasn't my place. And the notion of asking a lot of whys, about Gloria living on one side of town and him living on another, of an only on Monday night romance? I told myself that what Everett wanted me to know, he'd tell me. He was taking me into his confidence but was he really? It seemed to me that Everett was talking about a whole lot more than his penis.

What must that have been like, I wondered. From the onset of puberty, from the very first midnight surprise in Everett's underwear, his erection was always reliable. In his early teens he marveled at how great his erection felt. At the beginning of manhood Everett was ecstatic at the how often, at the how many, and at the how long of his erection. And how he intended to make use of it every chance he got. It was as if his penis was on standby all his life. Until last night. When it wasn't. So, this morning, his hands waving, gesturing, emphasizing, as he talked. Palms up, palms down, finger pointing and puncturing the air in the front seat of my Chevy Blazer. "When we get back to Spokane, I'm going to call the Doc. See if I can get this fixed." Determined to defend that special part of masculinity that defined him, that to some degree defines all of us. To not give up. To not give away that part of his life, that special part that manifests itself in that goofy Bee Gees lyric, "Oh you can tell by the way I use my walk, I'm a woman's man…"

We were hardly out of his driveway, heading a third time for Lenore. As we drove through the outskirts of town and turned on to Route 2, Everett wasted no time. He couldn't wait to tell me what he had been able to arrange.

"You know that problem I told you about? Well, the doc says I don't have to put up with it. He does these operations all the time and he's going to fix me right up." I glued my eyes to the road, knowing that there was more story to come. His surgery was scheduled in ten days, he said. He wasn't going to tell Gloria that he was getting an implant, I had to promise not to tell anyone, and he wasn't telling anyone else either. Only part of this was true. Gloria never did find out and I never let this cat out of its bag. But Everett? He told anyone and everyone who would listen, "This is what I'm going to do." His smile wide, his eyes determined.

Forestalling the inevitable was what he was going to do, I decided. I remembered the words my father said to me the day I was hired by Western Airlines: "It goes by so fast." He was talking about flying. About how long we could fly before the rules said we had to stop. My dad's "having to stop" was not too far down the road. The age 60 rule took the cockpit away from him in 1979. Different events, my father's sixtieth birthday and Everett's loss of potency. But the frustration expressed was the same. The disbelief the same. The anger the same. My father said, "I'm at the height of my powers…"

Everett said, "I don't have to put up with this!" The difference here was that my father's life was turned upside down. A page on his calendar took away the joy of cradling the controls of a 747 in the palms of his hands. But Everett? A simple gizmo gave new life to his penis. It was as if he was promised he would live forever.

Everett kept track of my trips back and forth to Salt Lake. He always wanted to know where I was. If I was home, if I was available. A safety net for him, I thought. There were other people he could call if something happened to him. But my impression was that should he need help, he'd call me first. The ropey red welt down his chest to his belt let me know that he had had open-heart surgery several years ago. He told me all about it. So, a phone call from his house to mine as I walked in the door after finishing a trip was never a surprise. I was a personal ambulance to the hospital.

The phone rang about a week after he announced his determination to have "reconstructive" surgery. Everett croaked into the phone, "You know that operation I told you about? Well, I had it this morning."

"You did? Today? Okay, I'll be there in ten minutes."

I found him sitting on his beat-up old couch. Rumbled khakis, suspenders, and no white T-shirt. Except for the ropy red scar on his chest, he was the color of fireplace ashes. Before I could stop him, he popped up off the couch, dropped the suspenders from his shoulders, yanked down his pants and said, "Look at this. All I have to do is point it up when I want to use it and point it down to put it away."

I didn't want to look, but I did anyway. It's not every day that you see a dick that looks like it's been run over by a road grader. I didn't know there were that many variations of black and blue and greenish purple in the universe. Swollen, battered, and sore didn't matter. Everett couldn't wait to show me how it worked. He adjusted his new best friend so it would stand at attention.

"How'd you do that?"

I expected a pump thingy, but he didn't press anything. He just bent his penis up and that's where it stayed. Up. I looked at him and said, "Okay, I surrender. Come on. How did you make it do that?"

"The doc stuck a little tube in there," Everett said. "It has some oily stuff and little balls jammed in it so it's always stiff, and I can make my dick point anywhere I want. Up, down, sideways. It'll take a few weeks to heal and then I'll be ready to go."

"Have you told Gloria?"

"Not yet. I kind of want it to be a surprise."

Surprise? Now that just cracked me up! A few weeks later, on a Saturday morning, we drove north of Spokane to Brown's Lake. A weed-bottomed lake full of downed trees which stained the gin-clear water to the color of tea. Still practically transparent, just tinted tannin brown. Sitting in a depression ringed with steep, granite-faced hills. Full of mayfly and caddis and damselfly larva that hatched in the weed beds. Full of rainbow, cutthroat, and brook trout that ate an insect smorgasbord. A lake with the acoustics of an echo chamber. And bobbing in his raft on this hill-ringed lake, Everett announced to everyone on it that Monday was the big day. Except that it sounded like *thethethethe bigbigbigbig daydaydayday*. His words bounced off the rock walls, skipped off the water, ricocheted around the lake, and found their way to everyone's ears. At least a dozen fishermen from Spokane. Everett's secret was never ever much of a secret, really. Now, as his announcement echoed across the lake, it was no secret at all.

And Monday night? According to Everett it was supper, the unveiling, a shriek, small objects thrown, and then the accusation that he didn't have this procedure for her benefit at all. Gloria accused him of getting the implant so that he could chase other women. And then she chased him out of his own house.

I don't think I ever told Everett how much I liked him. How much I appreciated him. How much I had come to care for him. And he never expressed anything having to do with affection for me. I believed, though, that he knew how much his friendship meant to me. Because we shared time together. We shared lakes and rivers and streams together. When we overnighted somewhere, I always brought breakfast and dinner for the both of us. Not cans of Campbell's Tomato Soup and Nabisco Saltines either. I wouldn't have brought that stuff even if he asked me. Oatmeal with raisins and brown sugar. Coffee made in the goofy little percolator I found in a garage sale. Burgers and chicken and fish grilled over wood fires. Potatoes, onions, and little baguettes baked in this fold-up oven that sat on top of my Coleman stove. And hot sauce. Which he hated. But I always had it and always made a point of trying to hand it to him. He complained, told me I was trying to set him on fire with it. Then he laughed.

The affection was unspoken, but the words about fishing and fly patterns and barbless hooks and weather and bugs and releasing trout unharmed that filled the time we shared sufficed for the words that men seldom say to one another. Affection, couched in words that never came close to mentioning caring. Those words about everything else were really about affection. And that affection manifested itself in time. Time given. Time shared. Then an empty place where Everett used to be.

I was on a layover in West Palm Beach when the phone in my hotel room rang. It was Alanna, my youngest daughter.

"Dad, Everett died this morning. Your friend John Propp called us and said that Everett's heart just gave out."

We didn't speak long, my daughter and me. There wasn't much to say. I took a minute to call Dick Calarco's room. He was the captain on this trip, and we were supposed to meet for dinner. I offered up an apology. Dinner was not going to happen. I needed to address the suddenly empty place that Everett used to occupy.

A memorial service was held shortly after I returned from West Palm. It was conducted by a priest from my parish. Our church, the Cataldo Mission, stood a short walk from my house. I was so surprised, because I didn't know Everett was Catholic. I was also surprised because there was no coffin. Instead, a small wooden box sat atop a little cloth-covered table. Everett was in the box. The priest explained that Everett had been cremated, and even though cremation was forbidden for years, it was now permitted but was a rare occurrence at Cataldo. And it didn't surprise me that Everett was a rare occurrence at Cataldo either.

I looked around at the people who filled the pews. Cataldo was only this crowded at Christmas and Easter. Not so much the rest of the year. Everett packed the house. He had a lot of friends. I looked around as Father explained about the cremation, not surprised to see a little smile scrooch up his eyes. I had to grit my teeth to stifle a laugh. There were a lot of half-hidden grins and smiling eyes.

Quite a few people spoke, including me—my eulogy went last. And nobody brought up the obvious question. But I was positive that question was on the tip of everyone's tongue. I looked up from the lectern before I started to speak and couldn't stop the smile that lit up my face. The faces in the pews that looked back at me were smiling too. "What secret, Everett," I thought.

It has been almost forty-six years since my friend died. I can't say that I think about him every day. Though when I see the Boeing Binder, I see his face, a stubble of white whiskers highlighting his grin. I think of him when I pick up the old Hardy Zenith reel that I bought from his widow. Everett must have gotten the Hardy when he was in his mid-twenties. A classic English fly reel he treated like the Holy Grail. I take it apart and clean it from time to time, then return it to a soft cloth bag it lives in now. Much nicer than the Tupperware container that Gloria used to store his ashes, on the fireplace mantle in her faded sitting room. I waited no more than a second or two after she left to find Everett's Hardy, which I bought from his few remaining possessions, then grabbed the Tupperware, squeezed the lid to be sure no ashes spilled, and shook it. The BBs went click, click, click. Everett.

It's raining today. The wind is blowing. It's cold. I was going to take my 4wt. rod outside and try to teach myself how to cast left-handed. I shredded my right shoulder's rotator cuff in four places in a Pilates class but really don't want to have surgery. The down time is over six weeks, and for most of that time my shoulder will hurt like hell. And I want to go fishing. In June, in Montana, just south of Livingston, with old friends from Western, who think nothing of being on a spring creek from after an early breakfast until dark, until tiny flies disappear in the twilight. But it's too cold and too wet and too windy for fly rods today. So I decide to retrieve fly boxes from the very small corner in the basement that she who makes all the decisions around this place has allotted me. To rearrange the contents into Montana spring creek fly boxes. But my palm grazes the cloth bag that holds the old Hardy. I take it from the bag and hold it, this fly reel that is older than I am, but not much older.

Everett's name is scratched on the reel's case, the part that holds the spool and the fly line and the internal parts that control the tension on the fly line. I love that it's an old-fashioned Hardy, but I love that his name has lived here for so long even more. And I think about the operation, about the gizmo that transformed a penis reluctant to stand at attention into a magic wand that restored Everett's pride and confidence and self-esteem. At least for a while. I didn't know it then, but I know now why this is important. I've finally realized that aging is about adapting to loss, to accepting that ever increasing catalog of what I'm unable to do. Some of those things are so much harder to accept than others. Like having to leave big Boeings, having my knees rebel against the pounding that running inflicted on them, on a heart that is tired. But none of these compare with the crushing anguish that comes with the fear, as Everett so forthrightly put this, of not being "able to perform." And I understand now what I didn't understand then about what Everett was trying to do. He was holding on for dear life. He realized that any remedy was better than no remedy at all. I think this is what I have come to understand. That needing her should never be surrendered, wanting her should never be ignored. And reaching for her? I cannot conceive of not reaching.

Chapter 13

Nelson's Spring Creek

Livingston, Montana, June 8, 2024

It's hard! It's hard when the breeze is up, to control the wispy strands of monofilament that need to pass through the tiny eye of a size twenty hook. Half the size of my pinky fingernail. That's how small our flies are. Blue Winged Olive mayflies. The breeze teases my now arthritic fingers, making the monofilament tippet hard to trap between my thumb and index finger, then thread through the fly hook's eye and twist into a clinch knot. But this has to be done if I want to fish this amazingly clear stream. It is full of large rainbow trout that sip these little mayflies from the creek's surface film. The flies I've tied have to be tiny, have to look like real mayflies, and have to be presented on an impossibly thin tippet. I sit on a log near the stream's bank. My spools of tippet and fly boxes are at my feet, and I almost squint through my 300-power readers to keep everything in focus. I get the clinch knot tied just as Tim calls out to me to turn around.

I lean my fly rod against the log I am sitting on and try to swivel around enough to see what Tim wants me to see, but I can only see some of what he's pointing out. So, I slide my butt forward on the log, put my palms flat on the log's mossy bark, and carefully push forward and up. My right rotator cuff is torn in four places, and sore, so I'm being careful, but eventually I am upright, and I turn completely around. Tim is pointing to the east, at the Absaroka Mountains that dominate our field of vision to the exclusion of everything else. Snowcapped, gleaming in the sunlight, spectacular against the crystal-blue sky.

It is always like this when there is no smoke, there are no fires. This intense blue sky. I remember it from the first time I flew here, in the late fall of 1977, forty-seven years ago. Cold and clear, mountains wreathed with snow that flashed sunlight like signal mirrors. A flight so long ago but always surprising to me. From Salt Lake to Great Falls. It was a big deal, this flight. Because the wind was out of the northwest. We would land on runway 35, a little over 6,000 feet long, a short runway even for our Western Airlines Boeing 737s that we flew into these small airfields. For new first officers, which is what I was, you knew you had made the team if the captain gave you the leg into any Montana airport. Porter Ellis gave me the leg into Great Falls. I was flying into Great Falls, Montana, with a 15-knot left crosswind, and landing on a short runway. I was flying a 737, a Fat Albert, the first jet I'd ever flown. Somehow, I calmed myself down and concentrated.

"Fly the jet," my father told me, just before I took the check ride to qualify as a copilot. My left hand disconnected the autopilot as we started down. And his words repeated, again and again, in my head. "Fly the jet." Let the nose swing into the wind on the approach and use aileron to counteract the drift. Then, with a left crosswind, right rudder to line the nose up with the runway centerline, and twitch the left wing's aileron down to hold the airplane straight. Gear down, landing flaps, an extra 10 knots of airspeed for control, and find the ground with the left main gear by twitching the left aileron. The ground just ticks the left main wheel, and the airplane is on the ground softly and the thrust levers come back to idle, and the reversers are deployed and Porter smiles, and the landing is perfect and perfect is exactly how I feel.

Breathtaking! The whole setting. That's what Tim is pointing to. What makes this so great is that he and Judi have lived here for over forty years, and to this day Tim is still moved by what he sees. His home is in the Paradise Valley. The mountains are here, to the east. And Tim's wife, Judi, says that she can't conceive of waking up not seeing Emigrant Peak. They once talked about moving back to Seattle. A very short-lived conversation according to Judi.

Nelson's is one of three spring creeks in the Paradise Valley, to the east of the Yellowstone. Armstrong's and De Puy's are on the west side, close by the highway to the northwest gate to Yellowstone Park. Much noisier. Nelson's is populated by big rainbows that glide up and then slide back in the current, duck in and out of long, bright green weeds that undulate in a current that is steady but slow. There is no gradient here like a riverbed, no pronounced riffles that distort and break up the water's surface. The fish are wary and easily spooked. They can sense an old man stumble as he sneaks up on them. I manage not to stumble.

I have always loved sight-fishing for trout. Seeing the fish that I want to catch, figuring out what fly to use, what the current will do to my fly, and finally where to cast. But you know what I really love? The bright green weeds that undulate with the movement of the water. They wave, flow with the current, and when the current eases, the green tendrils relax. Slightly moving. Still sensuous. Still mysterious. What bugs live on them and among them? How many trout glide through them?

Casting to these rainbows needs to be almost perfect. So the unwritten but never violated rule is to never say "wind." The closest anyone gets is "W." Because nothing is harder than casting a 9-foot leader knotted to a 3-foot tippet knotted to a tiny fly that can barely be seen, when the "W" is blowing. Even a little. And the fly needs to land above the fish and just off to the side of its feeding lane. Close enough to see but far enough away not to spook. And if the fly isn't exactly the right size and shape and color combination, it will probably be ignored. If that's the case, I change flies and continue to try to make the perfect cast, because hope springs eternal. And because the green weeds that sway to the rhythm of the current won't take no for an answer.

***

When did I get so old? I bet I ask myself that question at least once a day. It's all I can do to wheel the recycling out on Tuesdays and Fridays. After fishing, George asks the same question. Except he uses "we" instead of "I." When did we get so old? As if making the subject plural eases the effect of aging on him. It's not quite as bad if getting old is shared by the three of us.

Too often I find myself sitting on a log, taking a much longer time than I'd like to control strands of monofilament in a breeze that doesn't give my stiff fingers a break. And, too often, the fly I am struggling to tie on to that skinny monofilament would disappear from between my thumb and forefinger and land in the grass. And so I squint, trying to spot it among the blades of thick wild prairie grass. I know I won't find it, but I look for the fly anyway. Because while it is a pain in the ass to tie it onto the tippet, it is an even bigger pain in the ass to clamp a tiny hook in my fly-tying vise and make it. So I look, ignoring the futility of looking. I need to look. Because if I happen to find it, I can forgive my stiff fingers for dropping the fly in the first place.

I arrived in Montana three days ago, flying into Bozeman from LaGuardia, driving east to Livingston, and then south to Emigrant. George was already at one of Tim's little cabins. He drove up from Salt Lake. George and Tim were roommates during initial training with Western. Tim said that on their first night together, he was poring over his flight training manual when George interrupted him with: "Let's get a beer." Tim tried to decline but George insisted: "Come on. It's seven o'clock, semester break." The only other bit of information you need to know about George was that he joined the Marine Corps out of high school and spent all of 1965 in Da Nang. And now? It feels as if we've fished together for years, but we've been friends for so many more.

We fished Armstrong's the first day, and after the first hour or so it became apparent that there were no easy targets here.

I wasn't surprised that it was difficult fishing, but I didn't expect that it would be this difficult. It was. Even though we all took a couple of rainbows on dries, the number of refusals, rejections, and snubs was just about on a par with the ones I received at my first eighth-grade dance. I pressed to make perfect casts, pressed to make perfect placements, pressed to present the perfect fly, then pressed to find another perfect fly. I could see fish, and they could see me, in the crystal-clear water, 19-inch trout, completely unmoved and uncaring, lacking in compassion, refusing to entertain even an inspection of what I floated by them. Sneaking up on them didn't seem to help.

It was late afternoon when I looked over at Tim, who was as perplexed by the fish as I was. Tim, with whom I've fished for twelve hours straight without so much as an "I need a break, Francis." Tim kept casting.

I looked around for George. He had his fly hooked to the metal "keeper" close to his reel, sitting with his back to a fence post, looking up at the clouds that floated by. "Screw this," he griped, and then parked himself and his book at a picnic table. "Don't worry about me. I'll just be here, reading my book, waiting for you to get bored because you're casting and not catching. I'll be right here. Reading. I'll be fine." I guess George expected we would feel sorry for him. We didn't.

***

There are rituals attached to this trip. Like crab cakes on our first night, in our cabin's little kitchen. Because Judi loves crab cakes and told me not to show up without them. I don't. Easy to make, so long as I do this at home and freeze them before I leave. Because I know where to find lump crab. And it's not in Bozeman or Livingston. While I'm at it, I make the tartar sauce too. In the late afternoon, on the cabin's covered porch, we talk about flying. Tim and George miss it as much as I do.

Years ago, I told George that the reflection of the cabin's ceiling lights bouncing off his bald head made it hard for me to see what I was doing, so George never takes his baseball hat off anymore. Tim's face is creased from Montana's weather, its wind-driven snow, its dry summer heat, and his hair is now snow-white. For years he hasn't allowed anyone except Judi to cut it. She cuts it very short, and I'm certain she puts a bowl on his head for a guide. When I look at the three of us, sometimes I see us as we once were. But now, more often than not, I see us as we are. Balding, growing shorter, growing thicker, hair once brown, now white. I look at the two of them and smile. Best friends whose faces celebrate the accumulation of years.

At dinner, it's Tim, Judi, their daughter Jessie, George and me. With George, Judi, and Jessie, there is no dead air. I try to slide some words around them but it's impossible to do. It doesn't matter, because I love this part of the day. Many stories are repeated, many of the stories we tell about her father, Jessie has never heard, all the stories that she tells on him we've never heard. Tim laughs at all of this but never says much. And Judi loves all of this because some days, when Tim hunts grouse and partridge or fishes for trout, she has only Emigrant Peak to hear her.

We're all aware of our calendars, all know that at our ages we're playing with house money, several years beyond our country's average life span. So, these days spent with Tim, Judi and George? I can't not be here, in Montana, with them. I remember speaking with my father, thirty years ago, when he called to tell me that he wasn't coming with me to Alaska. That he couldn't manage crossing the chute of quick water to the gravel bar we had fished together for over twenty years. I remember the catch in his breath, the sobs that punctuated his words. I don't know if I could make a call like that about the spring creeks south of Livingston. That's why I keep coming to Emigrant, to Montana, to Tim and Judi and George. Because I can't conceive of admitting that this too has passed me by. Because I can't bear the thought of these rivers and creeks, of this incredibly blue sky, of these friends, as only a memory.

***

I could explain to you the mechanical motions of how to cast a fly rod, how to set a hook and land a fish. I could talk you through the mechanical motions used to lift an airplane off the ground and settle it back down. But mechanics are almost robotic. They don't account for feel, timing, rhythm. They don't hear the music. It's what Mr. Weaver (whose given name I never knew), my instructor in the second half of primary flight school at Fort Stewart told me, to "Feel the airplane. Whirl around the dance floor with it." So totally surprising coming from Mr. Weaver. Silver-gray hair slicked down tight to his scalp, a pencil-thin mustache, and nicotine orange stains on his flight gloves from chain-smoking Camels. His head on a constant swivel, searching the sky over southeast Georgia for the German Messerschmitts he chased over Italy during the Second World War. A steely fighter pilot equating flying with dancing? I loved the paradox. And his words? I never forgot them.

Everett said the same thing, using different words, about casting a fly rod. About feeling the weighted fly line unfurl behind me. And how the fly rod will tell you, by the tug of the line as it bends the rod back, that it's time to start the rod forward. To me they were both saying that if the rod, the airplane, feels right in my hands, then I'm doing what I'm supposed to do.

And the music? It was always there. But it took me a while to hear it. One early spring morning, sitting in the cockpit watching the passengers walk across the ramp to board our 737, Porter Ellis had his side window open, and as he leaned on the bottom of the window frame, he began to sing, quietly: "Some guys have all the luck. Some guys have all the pain. Some guys get all the breaks. Some guys do nothing but complain…" When he turned back from the window, he must have felt me looking at him. Without meeting my eyes, he said, "Do you know about my son?"

"No, I don't."

"He was crippled in a plane crash. Hit a power line."

Porter said that his boy was completely disabled, confined to a crib and a wheelchair, unable to move, or speak, or even see. As he told me this, he began to cry. Me too. And I couldn't get the song out of my head. It was my leg (my turn to fly), and as we started down the runway Elton John, playing between my ears, kept time with the airplane. I think that from that morning on, I put motion to music. Slow music. Eventually love songs, which were always slow, sensuous, fluid. The way flying and fly fishing were supposed to be. No mechanical robots allowed.

Walking along a river takes longer than it used to take. I'm glad of that. I know that slowing makes me more aware of the birds and the bugs and the color of the water and the lines of foam marking the shifts in current. I like that I'm not in so much of a hurry to get to the next riffle or back-eddy. That they'll be there when I get there, and the walk to get there is a perfect time to remember. To remember the airplanes that I've flown, ones that George and Tim have also flown. To remember that I closed my eyes, just for a second, as the wheels broke free of the runway and the wings lifted me to a magic place that only a special few of us know.

And the music of the rivers. Rivers and the music that rivers sing. Music that is not just about fishing.

I hold a fly rod in my hand and feel its balance. The length of the rod offsetting the weight of the reel that sits below the cork grip. The rod rotates back, and the fly line chases it, unfurling and straightening as the rod stops, its tip pointing at where the two would be on the face of a clock. The rod bends like a bow because the fly line pulls it back. But my hand doesn't let the rod move. When my hand feels the tug of the line behind it, my hand starts forward. The fly line follows. The rod stops at about the number ten on the clock face, but the fly line continues. It carries the leader and the tippet and the fly to the target. Only when the line is straight and the fly is delivered to where I've aimed does my hand lower the rod, pointing the tip at the fly. And I, watching the fly to the exclusion of all else, wait for the fish to make up its mind. And when the fish barely breaks the surface film to sip the fly or creates a dimple in the water as it takes the fly or gobbles the fly and then jumps clear of the water like a Polaris missile, then I cock my wrist back to set the hook and finally smile. And maybe George or Tim calls out an attaboy. And I bet that attaboy is barely heard. This is the music that rivers make, the music that rivers sing. Music that is not just about fishing.

***

I cradle the yoke in my left hand and advance the thrust levers with my right. The engines increase from a rumble to a roar, and the airplane starts to pick up speed as it charges down the runway. And I listen as the pilot seated at my right elbow says: "Rotate." I move the yoke gently back to lift the nose to about ten o'clock. The nose wheel is off the runway, then the main wheels break free, and the airplane and I am flying. My eyes scan the navigation instruments and the engine gauges, and I listen to the voices on the radios and the pilot to my right, but the voices are not intrusive, they are expected. And maybe clouds in wispy slivers slide by the cockpit windows and the sun splashes off the windscreen, and maybe it is all I can do to stay strapped in my seat, because this is like a kiss that explodes my heart.

The connection between flying and fly fishing? Simple, really. Both can be so sensual. The flow of the fly line as it unfurls behind me. The rhythm of the cast dependent on the direction of the breeze and the strength of the current, the places where the fish are holding and the bugs they are feeding on. The feel of the airplane in my hands. Its balance, its unnoticed movement through the air. Because I am gentle and fluid in my movements. It is not step by step. It is what is sensed and seen and felt. Not a cadence, but a song, created by wind and clouds and water and fish and bugs and me. Like the green weeds that flow to the rhythm of life around them. Like an ocean of air and a horizon that goes on forever.

Reaching forward to poke a square white button to off, I disconnect the autopilot. Never mind that the "book" says to leave it on. I'm flying the jet. Not the book. The book doesn't know its ass from a hole in the ground. Ease the thrust levers back to control the speed and begin the descent to the airfield according to the required profile. The autopilot can do this, but I know that I can do it better. Altitude restrictions and speed restrictions and flap settings and headings, and then lining up with the runway when told, and then lowering the landing gear and slowing even more, and I do all this because this is what I need to do. And I need to do it perfectly because this speaks to who I am—I will never let the autopilot do what I know I can do better. Is it raining, and windy, and night-time? Who cares? And so, my feet are on the rudder pedals and my left hand is on the yoke and my right hand is on the thrust levers and my eyes are on the dials, gauges, and the landing runway display, and my whole self is given over to putting this enormous airplane so softly on the ground that nobody but me knows we've landed. Flying. Fishing. Hands and head. Ears and eyes. Chances to be perfect, again, and again and again. Music!

Chapter 14

Lola Marie Galletti

Stamford, Connecticut, February 22, 2021

Dear Lola,

It's snowing out. Big fat snowflakes coming down, not sticking yet, and maybe not at all. Today would be a perfect day for you to show up because you were supposed to be here two days ago, or so your obstetrician predicted. But some predictions are like weather forecasts. They sound good, but their reliability is never taken seriously. It was supposed to rain today. Instead, big fat snowflakes.

Let me take a minute to tell you about the morning your mother was born. In May, on the twelfth, in 1981. She was a day or two late. Just like you, reluctant to appear. I suppose she had her reasons. Probably because she was warm where she was, and there was no room to clean up or bed to be made and I watched her being born by C-section. I had to hang on to the side of the delivery room gurney. And then I held her in the crook of my arm. Alanna. In Gaelic it means "beautiful child." She was. She is.

The next morning, I returned to St. Monica's, at 3 a.m. With donuts. Back and forth I rocked her, your mother Alanna, and held your grandmother Janice's hand, until four o'clock. Then drove to the airport, got on a 7 a.m. flight to

Minneapolis, changed into my uniform, and went to work. Flying a big airplane. Your mother is a lot more responsible now. She makes her bed every day. Her house is very tidy. But her car? Always as hot as a sauna. The more things change, the more they stay the same.

I have been anxious for you to show up. To hold you, sing to you, say your name. Lola! Lola, Lola, Lola! Lola Marie Galletti. When your mother told me that she and your father Justin were going to name you Lola, I said, "There's a few bucks in the name Francesca." That would be my name, in Italian, if I were a girl. That could have been your name, because you will be a girl when you finally show up. I love your name though, Lola, your Daddy's Italian grandmother from Firenze's name. And I need you to get here. So that I can tell you things. Because time is not on my side. It's flying by. I intend the pun, which you'll understand eventually.

I want to see you as much as I can. Maybe every day if your mother will let me. And there will be times when I'm not home, when my Katie, your other grandmother, and I go away on a trip. Like to Paris. As soon as we can. We will bring you back a present, maybe a dress from Le Bon Marché. And a present from Montana, when I go fly fishing there in April. I'll bring you back one of my favorite books ever, about two boys who grew up in Missoula, who went fly fishing on the Big Blackfoot. I'd like to be able to show you my Montana, and the rivers I love. To take you to beautiful Paris and have croissants in the Place des Vosges. But by the time you're old enough I might be just about out of time. I hope not.

I want there to be days enough for me to tell you at least some of what has taken me a lifetime to figure out, to tell you about some of the things I've seen, to tell you about that which I love, and that which has made me cry. Some boys will tell you that they never cry. Don't believe them. When your mother told me that you had begun to grow inside of her, I cried. Because I had been waiting for so long for you to arrive.

Today's a snow day. A good day to come out and play.

I have been holding open the door to the world, waiting so that you could step into it. Holding open the door that sooner, now, rather than later I will step through, going the other way. So, one last thing for now, something I will tell you again and again, even when I'm not at home anymore. That my love for you, Lola Lola Lola, is the kind that lasts forever. Even when you are not able to see me anymore, except when you close your eyes.

Chapter 15

The North Star

Edgewater, Florida, December 28, 2008

My hero is dying. Everett Caryll and Dick Scudder are already gone, and my father's departure is imminent. He has only a few hours left. There is not enough time left for me to ask him the so many questions that I want answered. And even if there was, he has been robbed of his ability to answer.

He didn't teach me how to fly-cast. Funny, that. I taught him how. And he didn't instruct me on how to manipulate a clam rake. I did bring him clams, though. It was expected. In fact, never a good idea to show up without a dozen. Or more. What did he do? He showed me that good behavior was like my grandfather's tweed suit, tie, and bowler hat. The suit, tie, and hat might be stuffy and appear over-dressed, and maybe a little rigid, but it symbolized the right way of things. That was my father in a nutshell, and that was how I was expected to be. I found myself unable to be any other way. The difference in what my father asked and in what others suggested was that my father's words came with rules. Rules formalized by words. There was no question mark, no wiggle room, no equivocating, connected to his "you will."

Get all the information, tell the whole story, step up if you're to blame. Be responsible, be humble. Limit the use of the words me, or I. And finally, unspoken, don't disappoint you mother or me.

The medals, the Distinguished Flying Cross, the Air Medal, and the Army Air Corps Wings, that hung framed at eye level over my desk where I did my homework? They were the equivalent of his tweed suit, tie, and bowler hat. When I finally framed my DFC, Air Medal, Bronze Star, and Army Aviator Wings, I said to only myself, "Me too, Dad."

A pump pushes air into his lungs. It rattles a little and wheezes a little. His chest expands and then contracts. The breathing machine's tube is the only tube connected to him. Pushing air into his lungs, and his lungs pushing the air back out. I recognize him but know that this is not really him. He left when the stroke took his voice and his ears and his eyes and his smile.

Always hand-fly it, Junior. Autopilots are for cruise. Hand-fly it up and hand-fly it down. All the way to landing. That way you'll always stay proficient. Your scan will stay quick, your brain will stay engaged, you'll never lose your feel for the airplane, you'll always be the pilot. Fly the airplane. Fly it every chance you get. Because flying is finite, and someday you won't be able to do this anymore. Not because you can't. Because somebody says you're too old. And you know you're not.

I see him in his uniform. Four gold stripes on a black suit coat. Not arrogance or humility. More a surety, a self-awareness, a confidence in what he knows, a confidence in who he is. He doesn't hide behind his Ray Bans. They enhance his visage. I know who he is. I look like him, I want to do what he does, I want to be like him. But I don't want to be him.

Flying, the tie that binds us, the connection that keeps us close. The secrets that the air whispers as it speeds past our cockpit windows, secrets that are whispered to the both of us. Get lost in the romance of this, the speed of this, the grace of this. It is a dance, this flying, the air confides. Listen to the music the engine sings. And dance across the sky with the magic that is this machine. It will do exactly as you say, so say to yourself that this flying will be soft, sensuous, fluid, serene. It will be perfect. He calls it a job when he tells me that this flying is the greatest job in the world. I know what he means. I know he doesn't mean to say "job." He means to say "joy."

I fly from New York to Orlando and drive to Edgewater, just south of Daytona. It is a dismal afternoon, this December 28th, in 2008. This would be my last day with him. This would be his last day with us.

Only his chest moves. Otherwise, he is still. The only sound is that one the breathing machine makes, it rattles a rattle that is terribly sad. Because as I look at him, I realize that I see him, but I don't want to see this version of him. Tied to a machine that will keep him alive until he runs out of fuel. Because there is no feeding tube. Just an air hose. Upsetting as I kneel next to the pallet he lies on. His hand is dry and cool as I hold it. A hand that will get cooler as the day goes on. There is only one thing I really want to tell him, but I save this because I want those words to be my last to him. I rub my eyes and begin the words.

"Thank you for everything. For insisting that I attend Chaminade and U.S.F. Schools you and Mom chose. For never allowing me to be late for anything. For finishing. No matter what it was that needed to be finished. For never allowing me to quit. For respecting my decision about the Army and going to war and then flying in it even though it made you angry. For giving me enough rope to hang myself and not interfering when it looked like I was going to. Thank you for giving me a great life. I should have told you this long ago." And then, the one last thing.

"I love you, Ace."

His engine will idle until it stalls out. And then what was once my Athair, my father, will be called by Naomhs, saints, and Aingeals, angels, to Neamh, heaven, to Dhia, God. It is one o'clock in the morning. The phone rings. It doesn't wake me because I have been awake, waiting for it. My brother Glenn says, "Dad died about an hour ago." A long pause with no other words by either of us. He sobs and hangs up.

I pull on my jeans, Bean boots, and a parka, and go outside. Clear and cold, this winter night, with some stars despite the ambient light. I know where to look in the night sky. Find the Big Dipper, use its handle to point to the North Star, the navigator, the heart of a moral compass, a compass passed on to me from Everett Caryl and Richard Scudder, and now to me from my father, from Francis John O'Dochartaigh. A way of living passed on to me by men who struggled sometimes to live by it but never stopped trying. Men who loved women who were smarter than they were, which was why they loved them. Men who had tempers. Men who loved, who were sometimes led astray by love. Men who could be thoughtless or selfish, but who later made amends. Men who cried. Men who tried again. Men who showed me that there was no such thing as not trying, again and again and again.

Chapter 16

V1

La Guardia Airport, May 1956

Arched windows go from the belt course that forms the base of the building's crown right to the crown's very top. The crown seems to mimic the same curve that defines the windows. And the windows, at this time of day, reflect the sun. Which reinvents their glass faces from transparent panes into mirrors. I am not looking up at them. Rather, I am looking right at them. Sideways. Over the copilot's shoulder. Out his side window. At the Chrysler Building. This is my view today, a magic picture of a magic building. This is a day that defines my life. I am 12 years old. But today I know.

We are flying north, up the mouth of the Hudson River. Manhattan is below us on the right. I am listening to men talking on radios. Talking to other airplanes, talking to the airplane we're in. I look out the front of us, over my father's shoulder, but then out to the right, back and forth, at New York's skyline, then out in front of us again. There are other airplanes in line ahead us. They are going the same place we are. To LaGuardia. When we land, this day will be over. But the promise I make to myself never goes away, and the love of this has never been over.

I've been to New York City with my mother and father. To the Museum of Natural History, to the Bronx Zoo, to *The Nutcracker*, to Little Italy. But this is another world. Looking at the skyline from the top down. And today, the windows at the top of the Chrysler Building will always be connected to the answer kids are always asked: What do you want to be when you grow up? My mother thinks I should become a teacher. Just not a math teacher. My father tells me he thinks I'd make a great architect. But the military? My father believes that men who stay in the military stay there because they can't do anything else. Or the priesthood? That would have sent them both into orbit. I may go to Catholic schools from kindergarten through college, but my parents consider religion as seriously as they take the rhythm method of birth control. They laugh.

Dad picks me up from St. Pat's just before 10 a.m. I see him framed in the classroom door's window. I am out of my desk before he knocks. Book bag in my right hand, a wave to Sister Athanasia with my left, then out the door. In the car Dad explains where we're going, Columbus, Ohio, then turn around and come back to LaGuardia. Daylight all the way.

"Leave your books in the car, Frankie. Too much to see."

Good. Who wants to do homework anyway? Dad takes his flight kit from the back seat, and we walk to flight operations, where we meet the copilot and the flight engineer. All three go over the flight plan, the weather, the projected passenger and fuel weights, and the gross weight of the airplane. Then the flight engineer figures out the power settings for the four big engines and the take-off speeds. He calls them V1 and Vr. Then he looks at me and says, "Once we get to V1 we have to take off. Something breaks? Doesn't matter. Not enough runway left to stop after V1. And Vr is when the airplane wants to fly." The copilot collects all the paperwork and navigation charts, and we walk out the door of "Ops," into the mid-morning sunlight, and onto the "ramp."

This isn't the first time that I've seen this airplane. But this is the first time that I really look at it. A white fuselage that curves slightly up from the tops of the cockpit windows, that slopes gently down towards the tail, getting thinner as it stretches rearward. It reminds me of the dolphins that I see where we swim in Long Island Sound. Two red stripes run from just beneath the cockpit windows all the way back to the three white oval tails. They have red stripes too. And "Trans World Airlines" is spelled out above the passenger windows. Two big engines with three-bladed props are mounted on each wing. And there is a boarding stair pushed up to the forward entry door. My dad and his crew continue toward the Lockheed Constellation. But I stop. Just for a second. "It is beautiful," I whisper.

Flight kits are stowed, pre-flight inspections and checklists are read, seat belts are fastened, and we are waiting for clearance from a voice over the radio named ground control to give us permission to start the engines. I am sitting directly behind Dad. He's in the left seat, the copilot is in the right, and between them is a console with four long levers that the flight engineer tells me are throttles. He is sitting to my right.

"Like gas pedals," he says, touching the red knobs at the tops of the throttles.

"Cleared to start," ground control advises.

"Cleared to start," the copilot replies. Red-capped toggle switches are moved to "On" and one by one, the engines rumble to life. Each engine sounds the same as it starts. A cough, then a slow straining to turn the propeller. And then a shiver as each piston compresses the gas which is exploded in its cylinder, and the propeller now spins effortlessly, exuding a kind of mechanical confidence as it throbs to life. Three more engines, just like this one, are started. The flight engineer "trims" the power settings so that the turbines sound as one. I am really straining to keep up because there is so much going on. Each cockpit crewmember has his own job, but they all check one another to be sure that everything that needs to get done gets done. No mistakes.

"Ground, TWA 812, ready to taxi."

***

We start to move. The flight engineer shows me a little map of the airport runways and taxiways. He points to taxiway bravo, says we'll turn left onto it and follow it to runway one-three, the runway we'll use for takeoff. My father is moving the nose gear to turn the Constellation. His right hand is on the throttles and his head is on a swivel. Looking right, looking left, looking out front, looking for trucks and baggage carts and other airplanes.

The copilot switches to a different voice, the voice in the control tower, and that voice clears us to taxi "into position and hold." Dad steers the Connie onto the runway and as he straightens out the nose gear, we hear, "Cleared for take-off."

I lean forward to see my father's left hand on the yoke, the steering wheel, his right hand on the throttles, and his feet on floor pedals that control the rudder. Now he pushes the throttles up to take-off power, the flight engineer adjusts the power settings again, and we rush to being airborne.

"V1," the first officer says.

I look at the flight engineer and whisper, "Can't stop now." He smiles and nods. Ever so smoothly the nose comes up, and then with a small tremble the main gear breaks free of the ground, and we are flying, I am flying, climbing over Flushing Bay, climbing east to the beginning of Long Island Sound, then climbing in a turn north and then west. The copilot holds a small chart that says, "Whitestone Departure" and points to the parts of the map that we are following. I look back to the front, at my father's hands and feet. The airplane is going where he steers it. It climbs when he moves the yoke back and turns when he turns the yoke. He is climbing this airplane and turning this airplane and following the chart's route. He's controlling this airplane with a white fuselage and red stripes and four engines through wisps of cotton cloud and over slate-gray water and past the west end of Long Island. My father is flying. And I am thinking that I want to fly just like he does, that someday I am going to fly just like he does, that no matter what else I need to do, I am going to fly because this is what my father does, and I want to be just like him.

New York's skyline is out the left window, now much smaller because the airplane my father is flying is climbing, and now New York disappears behind us because we're crossing into Pennsylvania and soon into Ohio, to Columbus. We level off and

Dad engages the autopilot, which will fly the Connie at cruise. Then he turns and smiles at me, "Waddaya think, Junior?"

And I say, "Wow." There's a knock on the cockpit door, and when the engineer opens it, one of the hostesses passes in lunch trays for the crew, and one for me. Napkins are spread on laps and tucked into collars. Stew on a tie is not a good look. As we come over Pittsburgh, Dad points out Forbes Field. The Brooklyn Dodgers and the Pirates have just started playing. Robinson and Reese, Clemente and Groat.

"Do you want to listen to the game?" the copilot asks. I look over Dad's shoulder at the ballpark below us at where Jackie and PeeWee are playing. On any other day, I would already be listening to the game. But not today. Not today. I need to watch my dad fly this airplane today.

A voice on the radio tells us to begin our descent and the autopilot is disengaged. And as Dad pulls the throttles back and lowers the nose, he tells me that he's not going to use the autopilot for the rest of the flight.

"I always hand-fly the airplane up to altitude and back down to land. That way I'll always stay proficient." I never forget these words. The copilot tells the radio voice that we're descending and then tells me that we're going to get directions to the airport that we must follow, that will keep us clear of other airplanes, then get permission from the control tower to land. And that's what the cockpit crew does. The only words spoken now are ones the pilots have to say to the voice on the radio or to one another.

Columbus airport is out in front of us. Wing flaps are extended as the Connie is slowed down. The flight engineer cups his hand and says, “The flaps make the wing more curved, giving it more lift, so we can fly slower and land.” Then the landing gear comes down and I can see a row of lights leading to the end of the runway. At the edge of the runway there are cows in a fenced-off field. As we get closer, they amble off to the sides of the field, only a few glancing at the noisy machine that’s passing over their heads. I wonder how many times a day they see this airshow. And then the wheels touch the concrete, and I barely feel it.

***

As we come up the Hudson, getting ready to land at LaGuardia, with New York out the right side of the airplane, Dad asks, “Look at the streets and tell me what you see.” So, I look, and look, and look some more. “The cars. Look at the cars. What about them?”

“Well, on some streets I can see the fronts of the cars, and on others I just see taillights.”

“Right. One-way streets. Not all, but almost all. You know why that’s important? You want to know your surroundings. Know where you are. That will help you know what to expect. And there won’t be any surprises. And you’ll know when something’s not right.” The copilot, who is flying now, nods in agreement.

Just past Yankee Stadium we are told to turn right, and we head east and then are turned again to the south. New York is on our right side still, and I can see the Chrysler Building. The sun flashes off the arched windows, turning them into a crown of almost blinding white-gold. The whole city should look like the Chrysler Building.

Out the front window is LaGuardia. It looks as big as a 3 cent stamp. We slow and the wing flaps are extended, and the landing gear is lowered, and we come across Flushing Bay and a stone bulkhead at runway two-two's edge, to keep the bay on one side and the runway on the other. The Connie touches down, brakes slow us to taxi speed, and we turn off the runway. We are back. And this day, this best day of my life day, this is a day that I will relive over and over again. The passengers go out the forward door and down the stairs and across the ramp and into the terminal. We go down the stairs and across the ramp and into flight ops. Dad signs some paperwork, and we walk to our car. I turn around and look back at the door we just came through. I can't see the airplane anymore. It's parked on the other side of the terminal. But I can feel it. I know where it is. My father flew it, and I watched him do it. I watched him all day.

***

"Look at the streets and tell me what you see." I remember, and so I do. I look at everything, and then, driving from Kennedy on the way home to New Canaan, I call my father and tell him about what I have been so lucky to see. Like the morning when the Seine is out my side of the cockpit and it is a clear morning, and I am looking down at "La Tour Eiffel" and I call him and tell him how Paris spread out almost to the horizon. Or how the sun flashed off the snow-capped Matterhorn on the way into Milan. Or how Shannon Airport Customs Inspector

Michael O'Shay, who checks the names of the crew members against his roster, welcomes me to Ireland.

"Ah, Captain Francis O'Dochartaigh is it? Your first time in Ireland?" He pronounces our family name just the way it would be spelled it if it hadn't been Anglicized years ago. And when I respond yes, Inspector O'Shay smiles and says, "Well Francis, welcome home."

My father's only question to me is, "Do you still get a free bottle of Jameson's if you have to make a fuel stop in Shannon?"

"No. We get 8 Euros credit toward a bottle of booze every time we come to Shannon."

"You do?"

"We do. Every time we land in Shannon."

"When do you go back?"

"Probably in a day or two."

"Well, would you bring me a bottle of Jameson's and a bottle of Courvoisier?"

"Of course. And my treat." I'm laughing, because I know that this is exactly what he would ask. My father once told me, while salmon fishing in Alaska, that he wanted everything that was packed into my fly box. This is the way things work for him and extends way beyond the flies I tie. If I have it, he is entitled to it. Period.

***

"Delta One-Five-Zero, you are cleared for take-off." The landing lights are all on and two thrust levers are advanced.

The big Pratt & Whitney engines howl at this power setting, and the giant jet begins to move, to pick up speed. The lights on the nose gear illuminate the runway's white center line, and shortly after V1 I ease the nose wheels up. The Boeing 767-400 follows, and Lima's runway slips away, now below and then behind us. We head north, parallelling Peru's coastline, climbing to 35,000 feet over the Pacific Ocean, heading toward the Equator. The autopilot is not engaged. When we level off at cruise I'll engage it. But not until then. And then grudgingly, and only until we reach our descent point.

It will take seven hours to reach Atlanta. The last few hours in all the hours it takes to fill up four years in airplanes that spell out "United States Army" on a fuselage decorated by a bullet hole or two, and thirty-two years of hours in airplanes that have "Western Airlines" and then "Delta Airlines" written above their passenger windows. My left hand rests softly on the yoke, the steering wheel. The autopilot is flying but my hands have cradled a yoke like this for so long, and I can't believe that in seven hours they never will again.

We cross the Equator and then Central America and then the Gulf of Mexico. And as we pass to the east of New Orleans, we are given a clearance to begin our descent, and directions to get us in line for our approach into Hartsfield. And now I ask the first officer to disengage the autopilot. And I begin my ending, the last ticks of a clock that has kept this time for thirty-six years. My thirty-six years. Years that define me, that say, "This is part of who I am."

And we fly our assigned clearance to the airfield and follow the airplanes in front of us. And intercept the localizer, a radio beam that takes us straight at runway two-seven, and the glideslope, which directs our path down to the runway's touchdown zone. The yoke is softly held by my left hand, and my right hand rests lightly on the thrust levers' red knobs. The morning air is smooth, and the airplane feels like it is flowing into the turns we make, and then I call for the landing gear to be lowered. The first officer moves the gear handle into the down position, the airplane is slowed to just a little faster than the computed touchdown speed, and we are cleared to land. The right main gear touches the runway first, and then the left. We are on the ground. And so gently that only the first officer and I know it.

We taxi to our gate and when the ground guide crosses his red wands in a X above his head, I set the parking brake, and the first officer shuts the engines down. Then his hand is on my shoulder, and he says, "I've got the rest of this, Frank. Leave if you need to." I wipe my eyes, collect my flight kit and suitcase, thank the first officer for saving me from having to explain the tears, and get off before anyone else.

The flight back to New York is full, so I ride in the cockpit to LaGuardia. As we taxi out to the runway, we pass the 767-400 I just parked at its gate. I can't look at it. Riding on the jump seat to New York, watching others do what I am now forbidden to do, is almost unbearable. And of course, LaGuardia's landing pattern is north along the Hudson, past the blank space where the Twin Towers used to be. I can see the Chrysler Building, but the sky is overcast and there is no sun to make the arched windows flash white and gold, and as we come around over Yankee Stadium there is no game today. It's the end of November, and Flushing Bay is a cold slate gray.

Chapter 17

Pathet Lao

Kontum, February 1970

The village is quiet. Silent. A stillness so unusual. Almost eerie. If these people are Pathet Lao, they should be shooting. We should be seeing the tracers streaking green as they come up at us. We should be hearing a .51 *ka-chunking* away at us. Rounds should be making snapping sounds as they whiz past our open windows. They're not. No green streaks, no *ka-chunking*, no snaps. I feel Michael Buckland move in the back seat, shifting from side to side, aiming the big telephoto lens out the back windows. I rock the airplane's wings in rhythm with him, Dutch rolling so that he can photograph as much of the village as quickly he can.

As we began our pass over the hooches, people stepped out from their doorways to look up at us. No weapons pointed. Only eyes. Women's eyes, children's eyes. The eyes of a few stooped old men. No young husbands. No older boys. Just women and children and stooped old men, their faces turned skyward, their eyes looking into the drizzle and mist, at us, as we pass over them.

***

The gray ceiling is only a few hundred feet above me, barely discernable in the pre-dawn light, as Michael and I hustle down Kontum's runway, break free of the ground and head west. West toward Dak To, west toward Laos, west toward this sleepy village where the Pathet Lao are supposed to be.

The morning mist eases off, but clouds still shroud the mountains, and wispy clouds called virga dangle from the slate-colored overcast. Virga are like sucker punches. These clouds appear to be harmless tendrils of spiders' webs but get too close and the turbulence that created them will pound the crap out of me and Bucky and my Bird Dog.

"Hey Michael, no napping this morning. Keep your eyes open, buddy. I need you to help me navigate. I'll try to stay above the canopy as much as I can, but turning through these valleys is going to make it harder to get to where we need to get to. I'll be looking outside so that we don't smack into a hill, and you keep up with the map so that we find our way to where this *ville* is supposed to be, okay?"

"I've already got my map out, Frank. So far so good. Who could sleep through this anyway? It's like we're flying around in a washing machine."

"I'll try to be gentler."

"No, you won't."

Our maps are big, plastic-covered, and topographical. Grease-pencil marks indicate where we're trying to go. This is the kind of map that an infantry officer would use, not an aviation map like the kind we used in flight school, a low-altitude chart which would depict airways. No airways, just mountains, skinny valleys, and jungle. So, I look out the window, cross-check against the airplane's compass, hunt for familiar places on the ground that I already know, dead-reckon, keep my fingers crossed, and say a lot of Hail Marys.

The green of the trees makes the mountains appear more benign. The green is lying. These hills are fingers of solid granite that can crush this airplane like an empty beer can. The clouds hide some of the mountains, and the green hides the rest. Down below, in one of these valleys between the ridges, is the village we're looking for. With hidden .51s, probably loaded, waiting. Are the villagers farmers? Our ops officer is certain that they are anything but farmers. We'll see when we get there. If they crank up the Chinese .51s, they're not farmers. If they're not farmers, they'll be on those guns as soon as they hear us. And all hell will break loose.

If we get hit? Well, not a chance that I'm jumping. I'm positive that this airplane will hold together no matter how many rounds it takes. And besides, we're only a few hundred feet above the treetops. Way too low to jump. A parachute couldn't possibly open before the chute and I hit the ground, so I never bother to strap into the chute that is between me and my seat back. Neither does Michael.

Along with everything else that I need to consider, I look for clumps of bamboo. If I have to put the airplane down, I'm putting it down in a clump of bamboo. Bamboo is rock-hard but it bends, making it less likely to rip the wings off the airplane. And it can hide me, my Bird Dog, and Buckland in its leaves. If I can't find bamboo, then a bomb crater is the next best thing. I can get slow enough to stall the airplane out, which means I run the airplane out of airspeed and my Bird

Dog quits flying. It literally comes down like a pancake flipped from a griddle. Hopefully into the bomb crater of my choice. And then what? Well, we discussed "then what" months ago.

Months ago, I said, "Michael, if we're ever running around down there, I'll be right behind you. You're in charge, okay? We'll head east, right? Toward Vietnam?"

His answer? "Not east, Frank. West. The bad guys will think we're going to go east." Michael says that we have to make our way to the Thai border, so we have to escape and evade by heading west.

"Thai food is better anyway," he laughs. So, he tells me to land this thing and get out, to remember to keep my weapons clean, untie my rifle from the door, and grab my ammo bag.

"Your survival vest has the stuff it's supposed to have. I know because I've checked it. I'll grab some Willie Petes [white phosphorous grenades] on my way out the door after you're out, and I'll have a couple of claymores [anti-personnel mines] in my rucksack." He tells me to stay tight behind him, hand signals only, no talking, eyes wide open, and it'll be okay.

***

Navigating through rain showers and being barely able to see where we're going is exhausting. And at any moment somebody could start shooting at us. Shooting up at us, and today, even shooting down at us. If the Pathet Lao are on a hillside they might be higher than we are as Michael and I weave our way through these jungle-covered passes. My airplane has never taken a hit through the top of its wing. I can't pull my eyes away from what's out in front of us to look for Laotians on hillsides, though. Just don't shoot, I mumble to no one.

"You got our position okay, Buck?" That's the other thing that has been nagging at me. We've been twisting and turning so much that I'm not exactly sure where we are. I always use time–distance–heading to get me close to where I need to be, but zigzagging takes longer, the distance gets longer, and the heading keeps changing with the contours of the valleys, so that for me this has become a big, fat, guess. Not for Buckland. He never gets lost.

"Start to let down, Frank. The *ville* should be coming up real soon. Just off to our left." We're not high enough to spin down onto the treetops. We're practically on the trees already, so I ease the throttle back and start a Dutch roll, rocking back and forth, gliding and rocking and sliding down from ridgeline to ridgeline, making us a harder target to hit, until we're dragging the Bird Dog's wheels a few feet above the treetops, with their leaves whipping around from our prop wash.

I see a clearing, just off to our left. I see maybe a dozen thatched roofs, right where they're supposed to be, and smell wood smoke. People must be cooking breakfast. Spooky, how Michael is always right. We're at about 200 feet above the ground right now. Perfect altitude to get a good look at what's down there. Perfect altitude to get our asses shot off. It makes me smile a little, because on these missions the good and the bad come in equal doses.

***

I flew with Michael for the first time in early January, and that should have tipped me off that nothing I was going to do while working for SOG, this special ops group, was going to be normal. We were sent way over into Cambodia to take Prince Norodom Sihanouk's picture. I didn't know that until we were strapped into the airplane, and I asked Michael where we were going and what we were doing. And that's exactly what he told me.

"We're gonna take Sihanouk's picture."

"Just us? By ourselves? No fighter escort? Nobody to pick us up if we get shot down?"

"Somebody will have to come to try to get us, but they won't be in the neighborhood. Don't want to give ourselves away."

"What are we gonna do? Fly down the middle of the street and yell 'Say cheese' as we pass by his front door?"

"Pretty much, that's what we're gonna do, lieutenant."

Who planned this mission? Well, the dim-bulb ops officer who was a major, and the intel officer, a much brighter bulb major, and Sergeant Buckland, the brightest bulb I've ever known. That's the way this covert group worked. Sergeants and majors did most of the operational planning. Captains, lieutenants, sergeants and Montagnard mercenaries conducted the feet on the ground missions, and lieutenant colonels oversaw the whole shooting match. What I didn't realize was the size of the role Sergeant Michael Buckland had in planning almost all the operations that involved my Bird Dog and me. So, I suppose that I'm alive because of him. And I suppose I could have been dead because of him too. The only consolation there was that he could have been dead along with me because he spent so much time in the back seat of my airplane.

Prince Norodom Sihanouk, who claimed his country was neutral in this war, was meeting with some very high-ranking North Vietnamese generals in a little hamlet in the western part of Cambodia. Initially the plan was to just bomb the place and kill him. But the plan changed. Cambodia was letting the North Vietnamese use the Ho Chi Minh Trail to transport supplies and move troops along it into South Vietnam. That's not being exactly neutral. And since they let the NVA operate from just inside Cambodia's eastern border, they really couldn't complain about us operating there either.

"Are there any commo wires strung across that street? Did anybody scope that out? Hitting a wire is a for sure crash landing."

"You look for wires, and I'll look for our prince. Deal?"

I'm flying about as slow as the Bird Dog will go, and we're so low flying by the building where the meeting was being held that I could have looked for a parking space while I was at it. If we were 30 feet above the ground, that would have been high. A few feet lower and I could have been caught in traffic.

Had I even unpacked my duffle bag and stowed my never-worn underwear in the wooden footlocker at the end of my bunk? I mean, I just got to Forward Observation Base 2, and right off the bat I was going way the hell over the border in an unarmed little airplane with a guy I barely knew who might be slightly nuts. It was on this mission that Michael explained how we were going to "escape and evade" if we got shot down. I needed to know how we were going to get out of here if we did. It wasn't important, right now, to know anything personal about Michael, like where he grew up or how old he was. This could be saved for later tonight, over what was to become my usual dinner of dehydrated vegetables and rice, because the mess hall was always closed by the time I got back to Kontum. Tonight, after more than a few beers, we could tell each other our life stories, but not now. What I did know about him was that he'd been running missions along the Trail in Laos with Recon Team Maine for at least six months, and before that was assigned to a quick-response team called a Hatchet Force. Sergeant Buckland knew how to sneak around on the ground without getting caught. I knew absolutely nothing about that. I was the pilot, and I was very happy with Michael being the tour guide. He was so calm and almost matter of fact about what we were supposed to do that it took a minute or so for what he explained to sink in. Sihanouk, Cambodia, several North Vietnamese generals? How much longer do I have to live?

***

"Say when, Bucky."

"When."

The last of the hooches slip beneath us but we don't climb. Not yet. I need to get the airplane clear of the village. Just because they don't shoot doesn't mean these people won't. And "when" means that Michael is done with the camera. And even if he isn't, Michael knows I wouldn't go back for a second pass. Never. The only rule my partner Phil Phillips and I have. "One pass and haul ass."

We broke that rule once, and our airplanes were riddled with bullet holes. The ailerons on Phil's airplane were severed by some of those bullets, and the photographer in Phil's backseat had his head blown off by one of those bullets. "One pass and haul ass."

***

"They are Pathet Lao, Frank," the intel officer said. Michael said nothing. I looked at the major and insisted again, "There were no men in that village, Sir. Just women, kids and grandparents. Not one soldier, Sir."

"They weren't there this morning, or they could have been hiding, or they'll be coming back. The Laotians bring their families with them. That's who you saw. And the families? They are Pathet Lao. We're certain. So tomorrow, Frank, your mission will be to direct the air strike on the village." Michael remained silent, but his eyes never left me. And when I looked at him, he nodded, affirming the major's words. I looked down at my boots. They were rotting from the humid air. Like a lot of things, leather rots from warm, wet air. The eyes that saw me today, the eyes that were looking up at me through the warm, wet, drizzly air this morning, will be gone by this time tomorrow.

A .51, a Chinese anti-aircraft gun, started hammering away at us. And small arms fire too. AK-47s. Tracers streaking green flash by my open windows. Snap, crackle, and pop. Like a bowl of Rice Crispies. Then a second .51, firing bullets the size of cans of Budweiser. It appears that the men and boys aren't absent now.

The sky lightens as the F4s, coming from Ubon, our air base in Thailand, streak toward the village, carrying 250-pound high explosive bombs. Snake. And 500-pound canisters of napalm. Nape. I brief the four pilots about possible ground fire as they approached, set up the direction of their runs over the hooches, over the plots of vegetables, over the water buffalo. I tell the first flight of two to drop "snake" first. And tell the second flight the same thing.

Lead comes back with, "Not nape?"

"No. Blow it up first and then burn it. Small arms and two .51s from the east side of the ville. Run from south to north with a west break, away from the hooches. Cleared in hot."

"Roger, SPAF. Snake first. Okay, lead's in hot." The lead F4 drops two 250 pounds of high explosives that split the world around it with its kaboom. And then the second F4, with its snake, the repeating blast making me scrunch my eyes for a moment. And then the second flight of two, one behind the other, snake first. The concussion from the repeating explosions makes my little airplane bounce and tremble and shudder. I hunch my shoulders, and wince. Then the first flight again, on their second pass, one behind the other, now with nape, and then the second flight, the same as the first. The snake flashes white, then flame, and the earth ruptures skyward, and the smoke billows. The nape canisters tumble after the explosions, erupting into an oily orange splash that turns the earth and the trees and the hooches and the animals a greasy black. The people who don't die from the snake are turned black too. And they are all dead.

Chapter 18

Finnegan's

FOB2, March 17, 1970

Today, nothing had changed. I took her picture from the back of the only book I brought with me to Vietnam. I brought Atticus and Jem and Scout and Calpurnia and Dill with me because I needed this moral compass to help me make sense of something that defied sense. Her picture lived between the last page and the back cover. I looked at her with her ash-blonde hair and her widow's peak and her almost smile and her hazel green eyes and her pearls. That it was a black and white photo didn't matter. I looked at her picture even though we had both moved on from one another. I looked at her picture because I couldn't forget her.

It has been four years since I've been home for this holiday. Four years since I've been in Finnegan's on St. Patrick's Day with friends sloshing pints of Guinness. Of singing "Danny Boy" at the top of my lungs but off-key, butchering the unofficial national anthem of the Ould Sod my father's family left so many years ago. Four years since I've seen Martin Feeney the bartender and Bill Clancy the bouncer, who every Sunday showed up at eight o'clock Mass still reeking of Jameson, and somehow managed to pass the collection baskets without dumping one in my mother's lap. It has been four years since I kissed the girl in the picture.

Today is St. Patrick's Day, and our mission has changed. It began morphing into something else as winter pushed into spring. And now we are flying all day every day. The war in Vietnam is winding down. Vietnamization, Westmoreland calls it. The Vietnamese are supposed to begin taking over combat operations. Except that for us, the war is escalating. Because we're supposed to interrupt traffic on the Trail through Laos and Cambodia, slowing the rate of men and supplies from the North into South Vietnam. A handful of pilots, a handful of Green Berets, a handful of Montagnards, tormenting thousands of NVA, buying the South Vietnamese time to get organized. Buying time with our lives.

Today is St. Patrick's Day and I am no longer a first lieutenant. I'm about to be promoted. Following tradition, silver captain's bars are submerged in a tall glass full of ice with a splash of everything in the bar except gin. I hate gin, so it remains on the bar, but I get to drain a glass full of everything else and catch the "railroad tracks" in my teeth. The camp commander, Colonel Fred Apt, will pin them on my collar, and I will salute, then go outside, out toward the bunkers, and make myself gag the booze out of me, then head for the same bunker roof I sit on most nights. The stars crowd the sky tonight, and I see her face in each one.

Today is St. Patrick's Day, and I think that maybe everything is about to change. The head of Cambodia's government, Prince Norodom Sihanouk, has been overthrown. He flees to Peking, and now Cambodia's ruling junta of generals proclaim the country a "Free-Fire Zone." Which means that if it moves, shoot it. And to give SOG time to get reorganized for this new version of the apocalypse, we have been given a two-day stand-down. Two days of no flying across the border. Two days of nobody shooting at my airplane. The only two days since arriving here that I have been able get to the mess hall for breakfast, lunch, and dinner. I'm not sure I want to do that. Maybe I have a better idea.

First things first, though. The showers are turned on, and the water is hot. This is the start of a good day. It's been a while since I've spent any time with a bar of soap. My boots are the only articles of clothing staying dry. The rest of me and everything on me is under a stream of hot water, getting soaped up. Trying to get sort of clean. As I rinse, brown water pools at the drain. Shirt and pants and socks come off and are tossed on a bench. Now me, scrubbing my skin until it is almost sore. I feel like the red clay here has been squished into the pores of my skin and it's never going to come out. I scrub until I hurt. I'm still not clean. Not even close. I still smell. My whole self still smells. And the Nomex flight suit? It smells like Eau De Armpit to the twentieth power.

Phil has beaten me to the mess hall.

"I have an omelet," I announce.

"I've already had two," he smiles. Anything I can do, he can do better, because for Phil life's a contest. Makes me laugh. I ask him if he has a plan for his two days.

"Sleep and Scotch."

"Nope. That's not a good plan. We're taking an airplane to Da Nang. We'll park it at the 18th Aviation Company's ramp at Marble Mountain, borrow a jeep, and go to the Stone Elephant."

We manage all of this without a hint of a hiccup. Beautiful cloudless skies through the Man Yang Pass and all up the coast into I Corps. Not much of a crosswind at Marble, a "Sure you can borrow a jeep" from the 18th's platoon leader and an almost good idea of where we're going. To an oasis of civility, of elegance, of white linens and silverware and China place settings. The Stone Elephant. Somehow we find it and walk in and nobody chases us away. It is a Navy officer's club. It's not Tuesday night, Navy night, the only night reserved for Navy sissies in their starched snow-white uniforms. We are officers, Army captains, who are wearing flight suits that will never get clean no matter how many showers they take with us in them. I can still smell us.

We are shown to a table for two so far in the back of the place that we're almost out the back door. But we're not, and there is a waiter in a white cut-away mess jacket who hands us menus and a wine list. His nose is slightly wrinkled, and his eyes are slightly scrunched up, but he is cordial and deferential, and he begins a recitation of the available "specials." He makes it as far as the rock lobster tails sauteed in garlic and little hot red chilis, served over jasmine rice with a white wine and Thai basil cream sauce, and accompanied by a bottle of cold Sancerre. And baguettes! The Vietnamese chefs are trained in France or are trained by chefs who are trained in France, and they make baguettes! We stop the waiter here. And Phil asks, "Can we have the wine right now?"

The light lemon vinaigrette salad and the Sancerre are gone by the time the entrees arrive, so we order another bottle of wine. And then the entrees are gone so we order two more entrees, and then two more. Pretty soon everything becomes two or more of everything. Three entrees are the best I can do. Phil? Five. And between us we drink six bottles of wine. Did we overdo it? Of course we did.

After months of C-rations in late morning and boiled rice with dehydrated vegetables for dinner, eating this was like walking through the gates of heaven with no questions asked. Remembering exactly what we ate that night speaks to just how fantastic the lobster was. And the Sancerre? The chance to have too much of one of the best white wines in the world instead of a can of stale beer was no choice at all. I looked at Phil after our first taste of dinner and laughed. Through a mouthful of lobster Phil smiled, "Beats the hell out of Scotch and sleep, Frankie."

By the third bottle I sense someone looming over us and turn to see a Marine lieutenant colonel looking at us as if we'd just insulted his wife. We manage to get to our feet, and Phil starts to salute but then stops. I just stand there.

"You are the filthiest captains I have ever seen. Who are you and why are you disgracing our club?" I have a little whiplash at the "our club" reference but remember that the Marines are part of the Navy, and I think I detect a slight smile on his perfectly shaved face. I say Bird Dog FACs and SOG and FOB2 and the Ho Chi Minh Trail.

And Phil says, "Me too."

The colonel, who must have known what all this means, looks at us and says, "You gotta be shittin me." Smiling broadly now, he asks, "Have you at least washed your hands before sitting down?"

Phil blurts out, "Faces too." The colonel walks away laughing.

The waiter, who would switch between being one person and then three or five, asks about dessert. We both say we can't possibly eat anything else. And we really can't. He then presents us with a final bottle of wine, and as he loosens the cork enough so that we would be able to pull it out with our fingers or, in this instance, Phil's teeth, he says that our bill has been taken care of by the United States Marine Corps. We pass the colonel's table as we made our way out, pause for a moment and both say, "Semper Fi, Sir."

"Semper Fi, gentlemen."

Somebody drives back to Marble. I think it's me. And we polish off the Sancerre sitting under the wing of our airplane. Then we wrap ourselves in poncho liners and fall asleep. All the garlic and the chilis that is oozing from our pores protect us from the mosquitos and scorpions and spiders and vampires. Not a bite.

I fly back to Kontum the next morning with a hangover so gigantic that every revolution of the prop is like whacking the bass drum that has replaced my head. Before we get in the airplane, I tell Phil that I won't breathe on him, and he isn't allowed to breathe on me. He is asleep in the back seat before I finish the exterior walkaround check.

Phil drives our SPAF jeep from Kontum airfield to FOB2. We grab our towels, soap, toothbrushes, and toothpaste, four cans of beer because we can't brush with river water, and head for the Dak Bla, where the village kids wash their water buffalo, we beer-brush our teeth and wash the jeep, and the Montagnard girls wash clothes. Topless.

Two days, two wonderfully quiet days, with a dinner still marveled at after more than fifty years. With a wine so crisp and smooth and surprising. Almost disrespectful to have drunk so much of it. But until now we weren't having much fun because people were shooting at us every day, and Sancerre wasn't our usual cans of old beer. So, six bottles? Why not? A hangover so prodigious that my head hurt when I tried to talk. A river full of silt and other who knows what, but none of that mattered because it was wet and cool, and the cool made the Montagnard girls' breasts seem bigger and rounder and perfecter. And nothing lasts forever.

We were back at it the morning after returning from Da Nang. Over Laos all morning and again all afternoon. And then dinner. Steamed rice and dehydrated vegetables and shrimp, with hot fish sauce on mine, but not on Phil's. If the sauce wasn't of the Nashville barbeque variety, he wanted no part of it. And beer well past its sell-by date? Painful.

Then Lieutenant Jerry Pool was standing in our doorway. Phil handed him a beer and Jerry began talking and his words took up all the space in our room. He paced from one corner to the other, making eye contact some of the time, becoming more agitated as he went on. Jerry's first mission, with Recon

Team Pennsylvania, was coming up in just a few days. An insertion into a nasty area of northeast Cambodia. And his adrenalin was building so that I wondered if he would explode before his launch. He didn't, but it didn't matter.

On March 24, 1970, Lieutenant Pool and his team were pinned down by a larger force of North Vietnamese. RT Pennsylvania was on one side of a narrow, steep ravine. The NVA on the other. Jerry Pool had turned an ankle and could barely walk. They announced Prairie Fire, which meant they were in danger of being wiped out, to Covey, the Air Force FAC who was on station overhead, and Pool asked for an immediate extraction. Three US Special Forces soldiers and their Montagnard team members, trapped on a rocky hillside, unable to escape. Unable. Unable. Unable.

I don't know how I knew. But I knew. I had a bad feeling about this. Classic Vietnam expression, those words. And I did have a bad feeling about Pool, a feeling that made my rifle 50 pounds heavier as I lugged it to and from the airplane. That made me lay awake at night, my eyes following the sweep of bright parachute illumination flares as they floated down to earth, swaying in the breeze, their light splashing through our windows. I wondered how anyone could jump out of a hovering helicopter into upright blades of elephant grass, crawl into the steamy wet of the jungle, and hear the helicopter leave, and then the helicopter gunships leave, and then the FAC in the Bird Dog leave, and know that you and several others just like you are alone on the ground, in the midst of thousands of people who want to find you and kill you. And so, you listen for a rifle shot, or a whistle, or a barking dog. Hoping you don't hear any of them. Praying you don't hear anything at all. Because hearing the rifle shot or the whistle or the bark of the dog means that people know you are among them. It is hard enough for me to climb into my airplane knowing that sooner or later the shooting will start, and I would pray that the bullets wouldn't find me. I can't imagine not being surrounded by the flimsy sheet metal of my airplane. I can't imagine the horror of a barking dog.

UH-1 helicopters from the 170th Assault Helicopter Company were on station, and one descended in a futile attempt to rescue Pool's team. The NVA groundfire was so intense that the pilot climbed out before he couldn't. And now Lieutenant Pool was begging. And so, "I'm going in," was announced by the flight leader. Now he and his Huey tried again. Somehow the team was pulled on board, the Huey began to climb away, and then it was gone. Probably hit by an RPG, a rocket-propelled grenade. The flight crew, the team, the machine. Gone. Shards of metal and chunks of flesh tumbled into the ravine. Some of the shards and chunks were burning.

I wondered about the announcement that Bikini 6, the pilot in the lead Huey, made. "I'm going in." What urged him, pushed him, compelled him? Was it the despair in Pool's voice? Was it an inescapable sense of responsibility to boys who would certainly die if Lead didn't act? Did that even occur to the pilot at the controls of that helicopter? I didn't know. But I had only to wait seven days, and then I would know. In seven days, on a two-ship mission way over into Laos, I would know that in something so immediate and so intense, the need to act is overwhelming. Think? Consider? Weigh options? No. Think about nothing else except getting to Phil. Turning him east. Making sure he didn't climb. Firing rockets into the .51s and AKs that blew Phil's observer's head off.

In the evening of the day Jerry Poole and his team died, recon men gathered in the non-commissioned officers' team room. A ritual began. A song was sung. A song about a dog named Blue. And squeezed into the lyrics was the name of every SOG man killed since this mission began. The first name sung, Larry Thorne, was the first man SOG ever lost. Tonight, the last name sung would be Jerry Pool.

Go on Blue you good dog you
Blue laid down and died like a man
Blue laid down and died like a man
Now he's treein' possums in the promised land

I look around this room, look at the faces of the boys in this room. Brave? Foolish? Bulletproof? Immortal? As I listen to "Blue's" lyrics, I search their eyes, and as I look, I become convinced that almost everyone here is sure that they are invincible until the moment that a bullet finds them. And then they aren't. They accept the probability of their death, the inevitability of their death. That acceptance makes the things they do easier. Jerry Pool is an exception. He was terrified.

But the people in this room? The people singing this song, reciting all these names? What is it about this ritual that makes me uneasy, that confounds me, that almost makes me want to cry? Is it the notion that death is an acceptable outcome? I think that maybe that is where these lyrics lead. That maybe the odds of being killed in Laos or Cambodia are an almost sure thing. And maybe because of this, the boys who have volunteered for this mission find it easier to jump out of the helicopter. Maybe they stop thinking about dying, and not thinking about dying frees them from the fear of it. And signing "Blue" is the key to entering Valhalla, a warrior's heaven, where the bar never closes, and the beer isn't stale.

Chapter 19

That Was Then. This Is Now

Southeast Laos, May 1970

A man was rescued after falling off a hilltop. A bizarre resupply took place on that hilltop, and a squad of North Vietnamese soldiers attacked that same hilltop with mortars. The next day, two of the resupply helicopters collided with each other. So a summary report of events might read: An Indigenous survived after falling off the Leghorn radio relay site; Vietnamese aircrews were paid for crossing the border with Laos to resupply Leghorn; at least ten North Vietnamese troops were killed attacking Leghorn; and a mid-air collision occurred on the way to the Special Forces camp at Plei Djerang. There were no survivors.

And the reaction. Well, for the man who was rescued I heard, "*Ban that may man* [Lucky you]." For the air crews who made money resupplying Leghorn, the reaction was the same. For the dead crew members in the crashed helicopters the sentiment expressed was "*Xin loi* [Sin Loy]," which sort of translates to English as, "Sorry about that." For the North Vietnamese who died in the mortar attack, "*Xin loi* motherfuckers." And then, in what seemed like minutes, these events on these days slipped into the black hole of "nobody talks much about this anymore." Taken individually, these events were miraculous, or funny, or sad, or vengeful. But they weren't taken as distinct, addressed as events important unto themselves. They were lumped together, acknowledged with a "what else is new" attitude by everyone who experienced them, who participated in them, or just shrugged their collective shoulders. Who simply soldiered on, who put one foot in front of the other, who didn't dwell on any of them for too long. That's what I did. I didn't spend much time rejoicing or mourning, even though I played a role in all of them.

Leghorn. That's what the Special Forces called the hilltop. It was a radio-relay base perched on top of a steep hill in Southeast Laos, and its being there drove the North Vietnamese nuts because they couldn't scale the hill it was perched on to attack the camp. The NVA could only climb so high before they ran out of places to stand. The next best thing was to lug mortars as high up the hill as they could go before they ran out of flat places to set up the mortar base plates and tubes. On this morning, the Kingbees, the South Vietnamese Air Force 219th Helicopter Squadron, were conducting a resupply of Leghorn, and they spotted the North Vietnamese squad as they were climbing the hill. That's why I was flying around Leghorn. I was looking for that mortar squad too. I think the Kingbees and I saw the North Vietnamese at the same time.

The NVA were just about set up, just about ready to slide the first round into the mortar tube and fire it almost straight up, with just enough of an angle to arc the round into the camp. But I saw them, and they saw me. They managed to fire one round, which sailed off to the side of Leghorn, then raced to disassemble their gun and take off down the steep path they had just come up. I raced to follow them, and the Kingbees raced to intercept them. They did, and about twelve men in green-brown uniforms lay twisted and bloodied and dead. There were no survivors among the North Vietnamese, because their bodies lay where they fell. Almost always, the North Vietnamese removed their casualties from the battlefield, so that only blood trails remained after the dead were dragged into the jungle. Most of the time we never really knew how many died and how many lived. We counted blood trails because that's the only tally of "maybe they're dead" we could get. Except for this time.

The helicopters returned to continue dropping off supplies until I interrupted them again. Now what was happening? Well, there was a man waving at me. He wasn't on the top of the hill. He was about 50 feet from the top, and he was jumping up and down, waving at me, yelling something I couldn't hear or understand. And he wasn't Vietnamese. He had to be Montagnard because his skin was burnished reddish brown from the sun, and he was not slight and fine-boned like most Vietnamese. He looked like a miniature bulldozer. One of the Kingbees exited the resupply daisy chain and swooped in to pick him up. I didn't see how they managed to get him on board. Probably threw him a rope. Or maybe the Kingbee was able to get close enough for the Montagnard to grab on to the landing gear and wiggle his way through the big open door. They landed on Leghorn's helipad, and only after the passenger was identified as one of the "Yards" who worked for the Special Forces did the helicopter's door gunner put his CAR-15 on safety.

The resupply was really funny. I watched each old CH-34 touch down on the helipad and off-load one box. Not two, or a dozen. One. Then lift off and head back to Dak To and pick up one more box. When I finished up that late afternoon, I tracked down Michael Buckland. He handed me a beer.

"So, what's the deal? The Kingbees made about 8,000 approaches today resupplying Leghorn. Each helicopter delivered a single box of something and then flew off to Dak To, picked up another, and flew back. All day, except for when we shot up a mortar crew and pulled a Yard off the side of the hill."

"Those guys get paid every time they cross the border. Thirty bucks for a combat mission. And 5 bucks I think for a resupply. So, one box at a time. Been that way for as long as I've been here."

"Jeez, if I got 30 bucks every time I crossed the border, I'd have a Vette by now."

"Mine's white with red leather."

"You have a Vette?"

***

Low overcasts make everything worse. Spitting rain obscures things we could run into because we couldn't see them, demanding low-level dodging of trees and hills and sometimes rooftops. It's always choppy just below the cloud bottoms, and a lightning bolt or two could be lurking somewhere nearby. The morning after the Leghorn resupply mortar attack Montagnard rescue was that kind of morning. Refueling for the mission they were flying had the Kingbees heading northwest to Plei Djerang, very close to the Cambodian border. For some reason that made no sense to me, two of their helicopters decided to climb through the overcast to the blue sky above the clouds. That was nuts because there was no way of knowing the altitude of the cloud tops, or if the visibility was any better at Plei Djerang. Or why two experienced flight crews elected to stay in formation as they started climbing. They never broke out of the overcast. Instead, they ran into one another and fell from the sky. When they hit the ground, the CH-34s burned. Too many engine components made of magnesium. Which doesn't stop burning until there is no more of it left to burn.

I tried to find the wreckage the day of the mid-air, but the visibility was pitiful. The next day I decided to refuel at Plei Djerang and used the time to and from the camp to search. I didn't expect to find survivors, and I didn't. Late that afternoon I caught a glimpse of a white ring near a tree. I had never seen a white ring on the jungle floor before. It was ash. Then a mangled, charred fuselage and part of another told me I'd found the crash site. With bent and splintered rotor blades. Blackened engines. And six charred bodies, twisted and burned beyond recognizable because of the magnesium.

Xin loi. This attitude was commonplace once, so commonplace that the phrase sounded callous because dying was day after day after day. That made it easy for me to breeze by catastrophes. Merely glance at them, spend barely a second or two of emotion. Like a crime scene on a TV show when the cop says, "Nothing to see here; move it along, folks. Move it along."

My voice from years ago, my voice, could not afford to reveal anything. Because I had no guarantee that the person listening would be around tomorrow to hear it. Or that I would be around tomorrow to speak. Very little of myself was given away.

***

New Canaan, May 2025

I wonder how someone uncaring and unmoved by charred bodies and blood trails could have ever been me. How did I bury this for so long? I don't know, but I did. Why does this bother me now? Because I think about Laos differently now, because I talk about the war differently now. My voice has inflection and emphasis, a lilt has taken the place of a flat-lined tone, a voice that years ago offered no insight into how I was affected by what I saw and did. I think about the charred bodies of the six Kingbee crewmembers now and am brought to tears. Because I remember the broken English we shared over the chatter of their door gunner's machine gun, and the snap, crackle, and pop of the NVA's .51s zinging by our cockpit windows.

Did I once shrug off, or worse yet celebrate, the dead mortar squad that we killed? That lay sprawled below Leghorn? I may have, but I can't now, because I am different now, older now, and I have given myself permission to mourn catastrophe.

I remember that my father, as he began what was to be a short journey into his eighth decade, cried often as he talked to me about B-24s as they spiraled in flames down toward the Burmese jungle. How Dad's eyes filled when he spoke of friends from later in his life who died and left him to fish the rip tide at Diamond Point by himself. How he begged me to come home for a while so we could fish together. And I often took my vacation days on Lloyd Neck, with him, and fished this place on the old Marshall Field estate that my father showed me years ago, when I was a boy, when he had just bought our piece of ground in Fiddlers Green that is now no longer ours but I still hold in my heart.

I have become the image of him. What made him cry makes me cry too. Because now, as I enter my own eighth decade, I think I see so much of the past more clearly now, and I think I speak about so much of the past more fervently now. Because I know my words are from my heart now. And there are things I want to say, and not much time left to say them.

Chapter 20

Last Words

New Canaan, October 30, 2024

Endings, final thoughts, a time to come to grips with that which scares me the most. And what's that? It's the not knowing what comes next, the not knowing where my words go, or who hears them. That's the hard part. The notion that anything I've ever said disappears, that my voice is relegated to oblivion. That my smile disappears, that I disappear. That's what scares me. That the end is really The End.

In Vietnam I knew that death was a possibility. We all knew that. And yet it didn't find me. It came close, it was all around, but it didn't find me. SPAF pilots who came before me? After me? They got shot down. Death found them. We were playing "gotcha" with our mortality. And "gotcha" was the real deal. Death's boney hand reached out to tap some of us on our shoulders, its toothy mouth whispering, "Tag, you're it."

I'm on the verge of my eightieth birthday. At this stage of my life dying isn't just eventually, it's any day now. Everything I can do is on borrowed time and has a much greater sense of urgency. I think that if I get to turn a page on my calendar, it's a good day.

While in Patagonia I considered that departing on my own terms was number one on my hit parade. I wanted to be in control, to call the shots, to bow out with grace. And for a while I was content with that. That was enough, I thought. And from that I felt satisfied with myself, satisfied that stepping the other way through the same door I was holding open for Lola was sufficient. I was wrong.

Endings. There have been endings that I never wanted to see. An end to the adrenalin-rush of combat. That was really something, that cat and mouse game we played over Laos. Leave in the dodging, just leave out the dying. If there was no blood shed, the game was fun. And when I think about it, how much different from this was the catch and release of trout?

The ending after over thirty years in the cockpit of a big airplane? That was painful. Absolutely life-altering. But life's horizon had extended beyond the war in Vietnam, beyond my hands on the yoke and thrust levers, my feet on the rudder pedals, beyond take-offs and landings. To Chile and Montana, to Paris and Provence. To Alanna and Justin and Lola; to Meighan and Colin; to Cassie; to Jamie and Elisabeth, and Anna, George, Henry and Charlie; to my Katie.

This life ends. This last ending? What happens next? How last is last? What if Nothing happens next? What if Nothing comes after Last? What if the only reality out there is oblivion? This is what scares me. I don't want to end, because I can't bear the thought of not being able to see my granddaughter Lola, not being able to hear my daughter Alanna, not being able to touch the girl with the hazel-green eyes, my Katie. There has always been someone to talk to, to touch, to hear me, to listen to, who could talk to me about what's next. Will I be able to talk to them, hear them, touch them, when the lights go out? Or do I, like Douglas MacArthur's old soldier, just fade away? What do I do? What songs do I hear? What words can I share? What thoughts become random? What thoughts stay mine? What becomes of me? What? Tell me!

I am not ready to write the last pages of my life's story. This is my frustration because I am not a fan of endings. I need to hear more laughter. I need to sing more songs, say "I love you" more. I'll even take more scares and challenges as long as they have happy resolutions. I simply do not want this journey to end. Not yet. And so, I keep putting one old foot in front of the other. And I hate the idea that I'll either find out or I won't.

Years ago, Uncle Diggie and I sat on Fiddlers Green dock after my sister's wedding, drinking Scotch, and I asked him how long it took for him to get past the war. He had been a crewmember on a B-17 flying from England over Germany. He laughed and replied, "Ask me again tomorrow." And then he said, "We survived. Your father and I survived the Second World War, and you Southeast Asia. Our survival means that we're playing with house money." And his point? That I should wring every ounce of joy from the life I am now privileged to live.

Because I survived.

Acknowledgements

The first creative writing mentor I ever studied with, Rifke Krummel, said that all good writing is about love and death. She was exactly right. This book was a lot more fun to write than my first book, *Only the Light Moves*. Maybe because the people in this memoir are people I love. All of them. In my first book that wasn't the case, so when writing about people who were world-class buttheads, all the old bad things poked at me, needled me. "Remember this! Remember this! Don't forget about this!" An operations officer who thought nothing of putting me in more danger than I already was. Doing it just because he could. A platoon leader who didn't have the vaguest idea what leadership required. A few of these people can be found in the first book. You won't find anyone like them in *When the Lights Go Out*.

Podcasts took the place of long phone conversations. Several were done one on one with young men who were recording our histories. With Bud Gibson, Fred Kroissenbrunnner, Zach Wood and Jason Collins. And in other recorded discussions I was joined by captains Phil Phillip, John Meyers, and Charles Ford. We were SPAFs in 1968 through 1971. On several occasions Sergeant Michael Buckland took part in the conversations. Three tours in Vietnam, all of them with SOG. We didn't know much, but Michael knew everything we didn't know. These podcasts provided insights I never would have conceived of myself.

The SPAF pilots who flew the SOG mission with me are the bravest boys I have ever known. Meyers, Phillips, Ford, and Doug Krout. I would have done anything for them in the short time we were together, including giving my life. I would do that now. We survived because of our devotion to one another. I'd call that love.

Two mentors from the Westport Writers Workshop listened, critiqued, suggested, and eventually smiled at the stories I've included here. Christine Pakkala has been with me from the very first class I took, in 2016. And Julie Sarkissian from very early on in the process of working on both books. Allison Dickins, also at the workshop, was a senior editor at Random House and Penguin. Her classes gave order to my work. Without these wonderful people my words would still be an unorganized mess. Not just mentors. Much more than that.

My agent, Ann Tanenbaum, is my favorite phone call. Hearing her voice makes me smile, and her assistants, Mary Noorlander and Kate Ellsworth, have provided a ton of encouragement and advice throughout this project. Always available, always ready to listen, always candid. And Ann? She took a chance on an unknown writer with no manuscript. Just a pile of essays and short stories. We've come a long way together, dear Ann.

Jean Williamson Carter has read and corrected every word I have ever written. Had it not been for her help I'd still be stuck on the first chapter of my first book. There is no way to repay Jean for her loyalty, her encouragement, and her experience as my English tutor. Because grammatically, I was hopeless. Thank you, Jean, for every corrected tense and punctuation. And for the where are you going with this, which gently nudged me in a different direction. And as with the first book, without you there would be no book. Thank you, dear Jean. We did it!

Renegades! My writing group. Minette Nelson, Collette de Jong, Rebecca Martin, Deborah Kasdan, and Alfred Vanderbilt. My sounding boards, my critique givers who never pulled a punch. Writers from whom I have learned so much. Teasing, soul-bearing honesty, tears. We started out as participants in a writing group. The dynamic changed over the last several years, from acquaintances to friends to more than that. I love you.

And finally, my wife Katie. My Debutante in the Woods. Who never misses a beat. Who keeps track of everything. You have given me the time, the space, and the encouragement I needed to see this second manuscript to completion. Thank you, my beautiful girl. I love you more than life itself. You are and will always be my only one.

References

The Go-To Books

Lee, Harper, *To Kill A Mockingbird*, 1960, J.B. Lippincott Company

McCarthy, Rebecca, *Norman Maclean: A life of Letters and Rivers*, 2024, University of Washington Press

McCourt, Frank, *Angela's Ashes*, 1996, Scribner

Maclean, Norman, *A River Runs Through It: And Other Stories*, 1976, University of Chicago Press

Vietnam

Burnes, Ken, *The Vietnam War* (Documentary), 2017, WETA/Florentine Films

Caputo, Phillip, *A Rumor of War*, 1977, Holt, Rinehart & Winston

Caryl, Raymond G., *Catkiller 3-2*, 2018, Naval Institute Press

Collins, Jason, *Pucker Factor: Stories of MACV SOG*, 2024 Volume 1, Issue 1, Collins Publishing

Collins, Jason, *Pucker Factor: Stories of MACV SOG*, 2024 Volume 1, Issue 4, Collins Publishing

Cowee, Bruce, *Vietnam to Western Airlines*, Volume 1, 2013, Alive Publishing Group

Cowee, Bruce, *Vietnam to Western Airlines*, Volume 2, 2017, Alive Publishing Group

Cowee, Bruce, *Vietnam to Western Airlines*, Volume 3, 2018, Alive Publishing Group

Cowee, Bruce, *Vietnam to Western Airlines*, Volume 4, 2021, Alive Publishing Group

Creedence Clearwater Revival, "Suzie Q," 1968, Fantasy Records. Written by Dale Hawkins, Eleanor Broadwater, and Stan Lewis

Duncan, David Douglas, *War Without Heroes*, 1970, Harper & Row

Edleman, Bernard, *Dear America: Letters Home from Vietnam*, 1985, W.W. Norton

Gole, Henry G., Col., US Army (ret.), *Legacy of Lies, Over the Fence in Laos*, 2019, SOG Publishing

Hersey, John, *A Bell for Adano*, 1944, Alfred Knopf

Hooper, James, *One Hundred Feet Over Hell*, 2009, Zenith Press

Karnow, Stanley, *Vietnam, A History*, 1983, The Viking Press

Mahony, Phillip (ed.), *From Both Sides Now: The Poetry of the Vietnam War and Its Aftermath*, 1998, Scribner

Marlantes, Karl, *Matterhorn, A Novel of the Vietnam War*, 2010, Atlantic Monthly Press

Marlantes, Karl, *What It Is Like to Go to War*, 2011, Atlantic Monthly Press

McAfee, John P., *Slow Walk in a Sad Rain*, 1993, Warner Books

Meyer, John Stryker, *Across the Fence: The Secret War in Vietnam*, 2003, SOG Publishing

O'Brien, Tim, *Going After Cacciato*, 1978, Random House

O'Brien, Tim, *The Things They Carried*, 1990, Broadway Books

Plaster, John, *Secret Wars of America's Commandos in Vietnam*, 1998, NAL Publishing

Plaster, John, *Secret Commandos: Behind Enemy Lines with the Elite Warriors of SOG*, 2005, Dutton Caliber

Plaster, John, *SOG: A Photo History of the Secret War*, 2022, Casemate Publishers

Robbins, Christopher, *The Ravens: The Men Who Flew in America's Secret War in Laos*, 1987, Crown Publishers

Sullivan, Leo, *The Columbia Eagle Incident*, 2021, Edith Lane Publishers

Veterans Writing Workshop, *Afterwords: Who Can Forget*, 2018, Fordham Westchester

West, Francis, *The Village*, 1972, University of Wisconsin Press

Wolff, Tobias, *In Pharaoh's Army: Memories of the Lost War*, 1994, Alfred Knopf

Rivers

Babb, James R., *Crosscurrents: A Fly Fisher's Progress*, 1999, The Lyons Press

Goddard, John, and Clarke, Brian, *The Trout and The Fly*, 1980, Lyons & Buford

Haig-Brown, Roderick, *Return to The River: A Story of the Chinook Run*, 1941, Willow Creek Press

Lingren, Arthur James, *Fly Patterns of Roderick Haig-Brown*, 1993, Frank Amato Publications

McClane, A.J., *The Compleat McClane: A Treasury of A.J. McLane's Classic Angling Adventures*, 1988, Truman Talley Books

Ramirez, Steve, *Casting Forward: Fishing Tales from the Texas Hill Country*, 2020, Rowan & Littlefield

Robbins, Chuck, *A Flyfisher's Guide to Montana*, 2008, Wilderness Adventures Press

Santella, Chris, *Fifty Places to Fly Fish Before You Die*, 2004, Abrams

Van Put, Ed, *A Flyfisher's Revelations*, 2025, Skyhorse Publishing

Walinchus, Rod, and Travis, Tom, *Fly Fishing the Yellowstone River: An Angler's Guide*, 1995, Pruett Publishing

Whitlaw, Ian, *The History of Fly Fishing in Fifty Flies*, 2015, Abrams Image